Information Technology for Masses

About the Author

Gopal Misra is a senior journalist, who has worked in some of the leading journals and newspapers of India and abroad such as The Pioneer, Times of India, Janasatta, Sunday Mail and Gulf News. While editing the Congress Party publications in the mid-eighties, he came in contact with the well-known telecom expert, Sam Pitroda. His close interaction with Sam convinced him that telecom and Internet are not only revolutionizing the media and business, the new technology would give new life and opportunities to the entire society.

He joined Siddhartha Ray, one of the pioneers in the field of telecom and Internet, who had launched **now-india.com,** as a senior executive. While Siddhartha discussed the various business models based on this crucial technology, Gopal Misra, set up a non-registered NGO, Asarkari Manch, to promote **Information Technology for Masses.**

The Asarkari Manch made a number of presentations before the key policy makers, which led to the concept of rural clusters with an IT backbone. This movement brought him closer to persons like Dr. Kamal Taori, who invited him to promote **Information Technology for Masses** in the northeast region of our country.

While Gopal Misra is keen to promote various convergence models for the media, he is convinced that IT will be a key instrument in unleashing the potential of our people.

Information Technology for Masses

A Key to Development of North-Eastern Region

Gopal Misra

CONCEPT PUBLISHING COMPANY, NEW DELHI-110059

Cataloging in Publication Data—DK
Courtesy: D.K. Agencies (P) Ltd. <docinfo@dkagencies.com>

Misra, Gopal.
Information technology for masses : a key to development of north-eastern region / Gopal Misra.
p. ; cm.
Includes index.
Contents: pt. 1. North-eastern region — pt. 2. E-governance.
ISBN 818069

1. Information technology—India, Northeastern. 2. Internet in public administration—India, Northeastern.
I. Title.

DDC 004.095 41 21

ISBN 81-8069-248-5

First Published 2005

Published and Printed by
Ashok Kumar Mittal
Concept Publishing Company
A-15/16, Commercial Block, Mohan Garden, New Delhi-110 059

Phones : 25351460, 25351794
Fax : 091-11-25357103
E-mail : publishing@conceptpub.com

Dedication

In memory of my father Late Pandit Trilokinath Misra

*Dedicated to my mother, Pratibha and uncles
Upendra and Raghvendra*

*For my dear wife Nishi, and our pretty daughter Roma,
her husband Anupam and their children Arushi and Anant,
and our son Camad, and my brother, Pradip and his two
lovely sons, Manas and Aditya.*

Foreword

During my innings in the Khadi Village and Industries sector in Uttar Pradesh, Mumbai and at the Planning Commission in New Delhi, I realized that our existing primitive system of promoting traditional handicrafts and rural industry could not really empower these vulnerable sectors. They cannot face the current onslaught of globalization. If we do not modernize our management strategies and marketing management skills, our economic ruin is near certain. Even our traditional exotic handicrafts and knowledge in herbs, food, etc., which in my opinion are unique selling prepositions, too will be lost in the present highly competitive market economy.

Apart from the present issue of surviving in a market-driven industrialized economy with the primitive tools of production and marketing, India needs to generate gainful employment to our millions of young people. As Sam Pitroda, a noted telecom and IT expert, has pointed out that nearly half of our one billion people are young, which can revolutionize our entire economy and make our economy robust, and provide them employment opportunities.

It may be noted that despite rapid industrialization and vast natural resources, the countries in Europe and America are facing acute unemployment problem. It appears to me that the only solution to this worldwide phenomenon of unemployment, perhaps, is to adopt the Gandhian concept of sustainable village and rural development, accompanied by a broadband IT connectivity.

The present assignment with the North-East Council (NEC) in Shillong has given me a new perspective to this challenge of economic development in this region. I realized that except for institutional finance, the region is not a neglected region. It is rather a much favoured area of the country, where our Union Government provides huge subsidies even for running the day-to-day administration of the states, which are not able to raise their own revenues to meet even the routine government expenses.

While offering this much coveted assignment in Shillong, my seniors and peers in New Delhi had put up a clear agenda before me to reverse the present day subsidy and grant regime to a self-sustaining model of development in the region. The potentialities of the people and natural resources have to be realized to achieve peace and prosperity. It is now quite known that there is a lot of resistance to this approach, mostly by those who have been reaping rich financial benefits from the grant and subsidy regime all these years. But it is also true that without empowering people to evolve their own sustainable economic development, they cannot survive in the highly competitive new liberal economic order, when we too have to open our borders for trade.

Since the north eastern region has vast international borders, we cannot delay any further the much-needed reforms in our systems. Is it possible conceiving any reforms in today's world without allowing information technology (IT) to play its crucial role? Therefore, IT has to be promoted in such a way that the common people should have access to this hi-tech telecommuni-cation tool. A modest beginning has already been made through the broadband community information centres in the region, as over 500 such centres have become functional in almost all the community development blocks in all the states of the region.

The Prime Minister, Dr. Manmohan Singh, has already announced India's "Looking East" policy. We are also a signatory to the Kumming Accord, which brings all the major countries in the region, India, China, Myanmar, Bhutan and Bangladesh, to form a trade alliance. I believe that it is a challenge as well as an opportunity to prove our worth in the emerging South Asian markets, where we have nearly 400 million buyers for our products.

During my nearly a year long tenure in the North Eastern Council (NEC) as its Secretary, I have travelled almost all the states of this region and have had an opportunity to interact with a large number of people, including academics, businesspersons, farmers, social activists and also civil servants and public figures. This area has very fine energetic human resources, accompanied with its vast natural resources. All this can be tapped, if we succeed in unfolding its HIPPO (Hidden Investible Potential Power of the Organization) and KIPPO (Known Investible Potential Power of the Organization).

If we continue to ignore these potentials, we lead our society to TIPPO i.e. Threatening Investible Power of the Organization. My initial studies and observations reveal that the lack of understanding of the ground realities of the region has now led us to the threshold of the FIPPO i.e. Frightening Investible Power of Organization.

I am getting convinced every day that our apathy and lack of vision for this region has led to the present state of violence. Recently, a study jointly undertaken by the NEC and the Indian Institute for Public Administration has reconfirmed that most of the NER is crime free and peaceful. With the signing of the Kumming Accord, this region is now poised for rapid economic development. It will have a two-way connectivity with the neighbouring countries of the South Asian Region to establish its GIPPO (Globalization of Investible Power of the Organization).

I have requested Sri Gopal Misra, an activist for promoting *information technology for masses,* to prepare a document, which may help our policy makers and also our investors to understand that how information technology for masses will change this region into a progressive business destination. The information technology is to be accorded its key role in this new development. But we need clarity of thought and approach to make our efforts more focused. The present publication is yet another effort in this long drawn struggle for development and re-establishment of the identity of this sensitive and vibrant region.

Shillong

Kamal Taori *IAS*
Secretary
North Eastern Council

Preface

The encouragement for writing this book *Information Technology for Masses* came from Dr. Kamal Taori, a well known Gandhian and presently Secretary, North Eastern Council (NEC). During his tenure in the Khadi and Village Industries Commission (KVIC), Dr. Taori encouraged various sectors in the rural-based industries, especially the hand made paper. If India is today exporting huge quantities of handmade paper, the credit must go to Dr. Taori's initiative. Before being elevated to the post of a Secretary, he served in the Planning Commission, where he played an active role in the evolution of the cluster-base rural industries.

Many of us may not be aware of the key-role being played by the NEC in the sensitive northeast region (NER) of India. NEC has been set up under an Act of Parliament with a view to coordinate various development needs of NER, which, perhaps, is one of the biggest landlocked areas in this part of the earth. Since most of this region is surrounded by international border, the NEC is also to coordinate various measures related to its security comprising eight states, Arunachal, Assam, Manipur, Meghalaya, Mizoram, Nagaland, Sikkim and Tripura.

India's eight per cent geographical area is in this region. Its population share is nearly four per cent of the country's total population, which is spread over amidst dense forests and hilly tracks and in the plains and valleys of major rivers, Brahmaputra and Barak, and their tributaries.

It is also a meeting point of the Indo-Aryan and Mongol tribes, which were living for thousands of years in isolation; totally cut off from the so-called modern ways of life. Over the centuries, people in this region have evolved their own socio-economic systems till the arrival of the British colonial rule. In the present-day democratic India, this region's distinct ethnic, linguistic, cultural and religious identity is being retained under constitutional guarantees.

Except in the plains of Brahmaputra, Barak and the Imphal valley and some flat areas between Meghalaya and Tripura, nearly two-third of this region comprises difficult hilly terrain. Therefore, it is natural for the people of this region to evolve their own system of governance, which is mostly in harmony with their custom and tribal laws.

In today's fast moving world, where the quality of life is defined by economic successes, the innocent sensitive people of this region find themselves at a loss. They realize that though in social terms, their region is much more advanced than any part of India they feel neglected that their economy is not growing the way it should be.

This sense of neglect has caused anger and frustration among the people. It is one of the main causes of the violence. It is also a fact that some outside forces have been exploiting their frustration to destabilize this region. This hurt feeling syndrome has damaged the self-contained economy of this region. Its share in the national economy has dwindled to two per cent.

To an outsider the region may appear to be on fire. The investors, whether they are financial institutions or individuals, hesitate to put their resources in this volatile part of our country. Instead of improving the over all financial systems, the Union Government has been trying to compensate this region with more and more funds through various government agencies, including NEC.

This policy has caused havoc and disturbed the delicate balance between the modern tools of the administration comprising civil and police services and the traditional tribal society. It has also been quite frustrating for the Planning Commission and the various ministries and agencies in the Union Government, that there was no commensurate economic growth in the region in spite of huge investment in the region.

At the social level too, the northeastern society has undergone a lot of changes in recent years. The liberal financial assistance has created a powerful highflying politico-bureaucratic class. Its emergence has divided the society among the beneficiaries of the system and those who have missed this opportunity to make considerable economic gains. It has added an element of conflict within the society.

In this process, the society has also lost most of its self-sustaining tools such as handicrafts, animal husbandry, etc. With the expansion of modern education, the frustration has increased manifold. Instead of trying to be a self-employed person, a large number of young men and women are seeking white collar jobs, which are just not available. It is estimated that more than two million young men and women have already migrated to various parts of the country in quest of meaningful employment.

Under the present liberalization regime, the role of the state is quietly shifting from the key role of a provider in the economic activities to that of a regulator. It means that the present system of grants and assistance from the exchequer has to be replaced by introducing meaningful self-sustaining economic activities This policy shift has unnerved most of the key players in the region, mostly politicians and civil servants. They still insist that institutions like NEC should remain mainly a funding agency.

This mindset among the powerful sections of the government and society negated the concept of a liberal economic order, where private players play the key role of economic growth. It needs an immediate change. They have to realize that the state has to reduce its role in various economic and financial activities to provide the necessary space for private initiative. The government, now, is no more the sole job provider. It means that the hope for a faster economic growth will largely depend upon private initiative. The Union Government's decision to earmark 10 per cent of its ministries budget to be allocated to the NER States does not mean further expansion of the bureaucratic order, but an initiative to reassert the Union Government's keen desire to make this region a hub of diverse economic activities.

With an image of a violence-prone region, few will like to invest in the NER. Therefore, there is little option but to evolve and empower local leadership to take initiative for their economic uplift. The government institutions too can be blamed for the present day situation. Instead of empowering the people to participate in economic development with their own efforts, they are being repeatedly told that the government would continue to be a provider for all development activities. Since the old policy of grant and assistance has immensely benefited a section of the political bosses and the bureaucracy, the resistance to the new policy of evolving a self-sustained economic model is natural. But the process of the much-needed change in the present mindset cannot be delayed any further.

During the tenure of Sri R.R. Shah, as Secretary, Information Technology, in Union Government, a deliberate and effective step was taken to connect this isolated region through computer and Internet based community information centres on V-tech platform. Some people are critical of these CICs. They feel that there is hardly any visible benefit accruing from the huge investments made in this sector.

However, the truth is that it has provided a broadband connectivity to the people living in remote areas. It is a quantum technological jump for the people of this region. There is a substance in the complaint that the CICs have not achieved their much-trumpeted goal in most of the places. But it is also a fact that despite initial hiccups, these CICs have made people aware of this technology. The process of assimilation of this technology has begun. It has given a new dimension to the region, where people have now access to a broadband, which is yet to be made available in most of the urban centres in the country.

With my brief experience as an *IT Consultant* to the NEC, I am confident that it is a great initiative, which is going to uplift the economy of the local people in a big way and may usher in an era of hope and new opportunities for the hard working people of this sensitive region. Prime Minister Dr. Manmohan Singh's policy of *Looking East* may turn this region into an economic powerhouse, which will be an envy of even the most developed regions of the country.

The book has been divided into two parts. While the first part deals with NER; the second part is about E-Governance and the key role of financial institutions like NABARD.

An attempt has also been made to reassert the concept of Sam Pitroda, the man who has successfully revolutionized India's role as a software world power, that information technology is not an urban phenomenon only for the people of Delhi, Mumbai and Bangalore, but it brings two uneven people together on equal level. It is a social leveler. With the high rate of literacy, northeast region is just waiting for a great economic leap to progress.

May 01, 2005 **Gopal Misra**

Contents

PART I

NORTH-EASTERN REGION

1

First Impressions

During my nearly 20 years of interaction with the North Eastern region, I have closely noticed that in spite of the adverse media coverage, most of the people of this region identify themselves as proud Indians. Soon after the Tsunami tragedy, which had hit Tamil Nadu's sea-facing areas, a number of young men and women from the north-east who had met me at an exhibition in Delhi were supportive of the Union Government's decision to meet the post-Tsunami relief work with the resources available within the country. Some of these young people even stated that Prime Minister Dr. Manmohan Singh's decision to decline foreign aid has made we Indians very proud and self confident.

It is true that the region has suffered widespread insurgency. There could be many reasons to attribute the causes of the strife and violence. However, being a student of current politics, I am convinced that most of the factors for violence have genesis in post-partition factors. Those who had signed the partition of the country in 1947 did not realize that the business and trade of the entire region would suffer, if this region could not have access to the Chittagong port.

Again in 1971, when the East Pakistan seceded from Pakistan and a new country, Bangladesh, was born with an active Indian support, the then Indian leadership could have secured some of the crucial benefits for this region. This opportunity was not availed. Although some of the top leaders in the then ruling Congress Party hailed from Assam such as D.K. Barua, vital economic interests of this region were ignored. Since the present day Bangladesh rulers have close ties with the much-dreaded Pakistan's spy network of ISI, this region continues to suffer. There are powerful mafia gangs operating border trade, and the demographic aggression of the

Bangladeshis has even quietly changed the basic population character of this region. Also, an unfriendly Bangladesh continues to help various terrorist groups causing financial ruin to this region.

In spite of these neighbourhood factors causing instability in the north-east, some initiatives have also changed the current tide in favour of peace. The biggest landmark is the Mizoram Accord, which not only ended the insurgency in the state, it has also become a factor to show how a peace initiative can improve the quality of life of the people. With nearly 97 per cent literacy rate, Mizoram has become a symbol of peace and progress.

Even in Nagaland, the peace negotiations have entered into crucial stage. Most of the Nagaland people now firmly believe that only a permanent peace can ensure economic progress and protection to their ethnic identity. It is now hoped that the Bodo insurgents in Assam too will soon realize the benefits of peace.

A new policy initiative is being formulated to shift emphasis to peaceful areas for promoting development. There is a suggestion that peace should be rewarded by offering special financial packages for faster economic development. It is now being increasingly appreciated that all our efforts and financial resources should be more focused in such areas, where peace and tranquility prevails. The current impression needs to be revised that various agencies of the Union Government provide liberal assistance and special economic packages only to the violence-prone areas. The Arunachal Chief Minister, Sri Gegong Apang, is quite bitter that while the violence-prone states like Jammu-Kashmir and Manipur receive special financial assistance, some of the legitimate demands of his state are being deliberately ignored.

The NEC, perhaps, too is keen to remove this impression. It has taken some corrective measures on this vexed issue. A joint study by the Indian Institute of Public Administration and the NEC in the current year (2005) has revealed that most of the NER is much more peaceful than the rest of India.

The tribal society as well as other social groups have an inbuilt sense of social responsibilities and commitments. They appreciate and cherish human values. Women and children are much safer even in the violence-prone districts of this region than the metros like Delhi and Mumbai.

If the people of this region can evolve such a highly developed social consciousness, which may be an envy of even the so-called developed society, they can also successfully adopt a self-sustained economy provided they are equipped with modern tools and infrastructure. The NEC's top leadership comprising its chairman, Sri P.R. Kyndiah, who is also a Union Minister for Tribal Affairs and Development of North Eastern Region (DONER), and NEC Secretary, Dr. Kamal Taori appear to be keen to evolve a development model based on local initiative. Dr. Kamal Taori, apart from being a senior civil servant, is also well-known for his commitment to rural uplift with the help of information technology. Both appear to be committed to use this modern communication tool for self-employment. Fortunately, the Union Government has already laid a sound foundation for the IT revolution by setting up CICs, but they are yet to be made the hub of local business and trade. During one of his visits to the NER in the first quarter of the year 2005, Sri R.R. Shah, Planning Secretary, noticed that the CICs too have become a part of the vast non-functioning subordinate government offices in this region. Since Shah, during his tenure as Secretary IT, had initiated the setting up of CICs in each block, he was quite dismayed by their poor functioning. In spite of these experiences, this writer, however, is fully convinced that it is only a matter of time, when the CICs will attain their mission as a key facilitator for development and self-employment. IT will modernize trade and business activities to provide an online market for the exquisite produces of this beautiful region. It must be realized that even in the modern urban centres in other parts of the country, it took years to put computer to optimum use. Therefore, this delayed and slow response should not frustrate us. But we may try to correct the present policy of CICs management. They should be handed over to private people.

The NER is passing through various facets of human development. Its traditional conservative tribal society is interfacing the 21st century world, where hi-tech has crumbled down the geographical barriers. The flow of information has also invaded this part of the world. A large number of young men and women of this region frequently use Internet. In cities like Guwahati, Shillong, Aizwal, one may visit a cyber cafe to check the E-mail. Both private and government initiatives have made a large number of people computer literate. A sound foundation for using information technology (IT) for masses has already been made, but it needs specialized managerial skills, accompanied with a strong professional push to make the local people realize that their centuries old isolation has already ended. They too are a part of the global village, where flow of information technology has cut across all the natural and manmade boundaries.

It is already a fact that in most of the BPOs (Business Process Outsourcing) in Bangalore, Mumbai and Delhi (Gurgaon), there is a large presence of young men and women from the north-east.

2

In Quest of Market-Driven Policy

It appears that the most of current stagnation and economic woes of this region may soon be redressed following opening up of its borders with Bangladesh and Myanmar. The present illegal border trade may be legitimized. But it may also adversely affect its unbalanced economy. The region has an underdeveloped agriculture, weak industrial sector and inflated service sector.

It is a real challenge for the policy makers and local leaders to improve agriculture from the present pattern of Jhum cultivation in hills, and traditional single crop farming in the plains. The improved agriculture productivity in certain pockets indicates that this sector should be tapped without any further delay. But it will need market. A smooth access to markets is one of the biggest challenges for this region.

The recent experience of Mizoram is an eye-opener. The state has been declared an organic state, which means its agriculture produce is being cultivated without use of chemical fertilizers and insecticides. Some of the leading hotels in the country have evinced interest to buy cereals and vegetables from Mizoram, but the cost of carrying the agriculture produce is very high. The products could not be sent to hotels outside north-east.

Most of the industrial estates in this region are sick. The much-needed industrialization could not take off. Similarly, the small industries are in bad shape. The new generation is not interested in the traditional handicrafts and other products due to low returns. It has created a growing chasm between the national economy and the regional economy. While the national economy has registered a high growth rate of nearly 8 per cent per annum, the regional economy has slowed down to a minimal two per cent annual growth rate.

The concept of smaller states to bring the government closer to people too has failed, as these states have adopted the feudal style of governance. They have expanded their unproductive bureaucracy. The smaller states like Meghalaya and Mizoram have a battery of secretaries to the government. This top-heavy administrative machinery in the NER states have become an economic burden to these states, which are left with hardly any money for development. Even for keeping the huge official paraphanalia these governments depend on the Union Government funds for their routine day-to-day expenses.

It is true that it is not easy to dismantle this large unproductive state machinery immediately. But serious efforts can be made to improve their functioning by reorienting them towards market-driven economic and development concept. They have to realize that the IT has to be given a key role in the economic development of this region. The state administration should be geared up on the IT platform. A humble beginning can be made immediately by creating an IT hub at the NEC headquarters in Shillong having connectivity with all the NER States immediately.

The prosperity of a region is evaluated on the basis of values and efforts of any society or social group to turn its assets into economic gains. In recent years, governments around the world are beginning to understand the role of IT as a key instrument of governance and business. Therefore, in this context, the setting up of Community Information Centres (CICs) in the NER should be appreciated. It is a quantum jump for this backward region to be on a digital platform providing it to unleash its genius on a global platform. But the state machinery in this region, including NEC, is yet to be on IT platform to modernize its vast government set-up.

It is true that the knowledge is generally an intangible product tacitly stored among all of us. The advent of Internet and automated E-business systems has provided a key hi-tech tool even to common people at an affordable price. Even without a personal computer, one may keep an Internet identity providing global connectivity. It is a common thing for an urban dweller of Guwahati or Shillong. The rural people of remote areas of NER may now have the global access through CICs on V-sat platform providing a minimum bandwidth of

125 kbps. The traders in the remote areas of NER have now global access through the CICs. But they need to be trained how to use this facility. Most of the CICs work like government offices. They seldom function beyond office hours.

There are a large number of texts on knowledge management using IT as the backbone of economic development for enhancing market activities. Although, few can deny the crucial role of IT as a key tool and engine of economic development it has to be customized for each sector and specific geographical region. It requires a thorough customized concept of knowledge and its management processes. Therefore, we have to adopt an IT-based economic development strategy accompanied with pro-active government initiatives. It has to be continuously updated and structured to incorporate internal organization, accessing and optimizing the available data for marketing both for local consumption and outside the respective geographical area.

Another crucial factor, which needs attention of the policy makers, is that E-business is quietly altering the present market scenario worldwide. It is dismantling all geographical boundaries. However, success of E-business in any respective area largely depends upon the level of E-governance. While the CICs have provided world-class digital connectivity to the region, the state governments are yet to implement the concept of E-governance. The Tripura Government has successfully implemented E-governance in various state government departments, but it requires media support for creating necessary awareness among people. Instead of appreciating the efforts of the state government, some newspapers, unfortunately, give adverse publicity to the teething trouble in computerization of the state machinery. The optimum utilization of the present investment in the IT sector in the region will only be possible, if NEC approves and recognizes IT as a key tool for E-governance and E-business in the region. Once this policy is adopted and approved in the NEC, the state governments and the NEC may jointly work to customize various schemes and development plans to exploit the CIC connectivity in the development blocks in the region.

The proposal to set-up knowledge platforms sector wise and geography wise to help the new entrepreneurship further strengthen this movement.

3

The Strategy

The increasing awareness about the digital divide has helped various local bodies in the USA to promote IT in their respective areas. The reason is that major cable and telephone companies see no profit in such ventures. They just do not have any plan to invest in connecting rural and small cities. In some areas, many entrepreneurial firms, mostly using low-cost license-free fixed wireless technology, have tried to bridge this gap. But in many places, especially the small communities in remote rural areas, even shoe-string entrepreneurs are absent. The only Internet access is dial-up. It is now being increasingly appreciated that this dearth of broadband is beginning to have a negative economic impact. Fortunately, India's telecom policy has already taken care of this factor. The concept of Universal Obligation Fund (UOF) has been created by charging a small cess on urban consumers to subsidise rural telephony.

The telecom players in the USA believe that the primary target market is small communities of 10,000 inhabitants or less. The Wireless Internet Service Providers (WISP) have already started focusing on small towns and villages. Some of the top telecom managers believe WISP may soon represent a huge market opportunity for the telecom and IT service providers.

The US experience appears to be re-enacted in the north-east. The setting up of CICs with an inbuilt system for offering a wireless connectivity in a five-kilometre radius has opened new opportunities for IT in the rural areas. But CICs are yet to be equipped with WISP.

However, the success of the IT-based development programmes in the region will largely depend upon the creation of a strong database accompanied by pro-development policy initiatives. The success will largely depend upon the creation of knowledge bank, improving knowledge access, enhancing the knowledge environment and managing knowledge as an asset.

With the availability of connectivity within a radius of five kilometers around each CIC, the much-discussed **Rural Clusters** now can be a reality. But a definite strategy for rural development will require customized approach for local people's empowerment, knowledge management and time management to maintain cost effectiveness of each product produced in the rural clusters and marketed.

The concept of optimum utilization needs emphasis in this region. There is an urgent need to implement the following suggestions:

1. The much-awaited IT hub should be made operational as suggested in the P.P. Shrivastava Committee recommendations.
2. A three-month IT-literacy programme for the entire NEC staff may be initiated for optimum utilization of the proposed IT hub.
3. The NEC staff members will be trained in such a way that they would be able to adopt a complementary role of evolving internal knowledge base to promote the concept of e-governance and e-business. In this process, they would also be made aware of the products and services already available in NER and the need to blend this knowledge with modern techniques and services.
4. The security aspects of the region may be considered while selecting a reputed IT company for setting up the proposed IT hub.
5. The LAN (local area network) system will add to the efficiency of the NEC secretariat. The confidentiality of the documents is a part of the LAN system.
6. The IT hub will be useful, if its installation is accompanied with a strong database from the states of the region. Since it will be interactive, setting up of the hub too will benefit the states.
7. Since Hon'ble Minister, DONER, is also the Chairman of

the NEC, the IT-hub will provide instant connectivity and information to the Chairman on a continuous day-to-day basis.

8. The **NEC IT Hub** will also act as a **Knowledge Platform** for e-governance, e-business. It will provide new entrepreneurship opportunities in the region.

If these suggestions could be implemented, IT would assume a pivotal role in the NER. The state governments too would implement various e-governance proposals. The CICs would become the hub of activities.

4

A Comprehensive Approach

This study is an attempt to blend various software and hardware technologies to evolve a role for IT in the life of common people. With the process of modernization and transparency, which is quietly taking place in NER despite resistance of subordinate services and other vested interests, the CICs will become the facilitators like telephone booths in both urban and rural areas. But these centres should be in hands of private persons, who have to make a living through these setups.

It cannot be ruled out that in some of the urban centres private ISP (Internet Service Provider) will give strong competition to the government-owned Bharat Sanchar Nigam Limited. The decision of the Assam State Government to allow the Power Grid Corporation to use the state government-owned power lines for providing internet connectivity will give easy and cheap IT access to common householders that too on a broadband.

With a view to assimilate the existing components in the proposed IT-based system, the proposed restructuring system is to be evolved on the basis of the P.P. Shrivastava Committee on the Revitalization of the North Eastern Council (NEC). It may be noted that the Committee has suggested a number of measures to improve the current working of the NEC to make it a really vibrant coordinating and planning agency solely devoted to the entire North East Region. But all this needs free flow of knowledge and information within the organization and a dependable connectivity with the concerned institutions—the State Governments, financial institutions, Chambers of Commerce, etc.

It is not for the first time that efforts are being made to make IT as the backbone of the NEC. The very fact that in 1988, NEC had already installed mini mainframe computers through NIC at its headquarters shows commitment of the then government and policy makers at the apex to run the NEC on most modern systems. A huge annual maintenance fee was being paid to NIC to keep the mini mainframe computers functioning. However, it is quite surprising why these equipments were not put to use and staff not trained to make use of this hi-tech system. The v-sat equipments for providing assured connectivity to the NEC are being wasted.

However, the following precautions may be taken while setting up the IT hub at the NEC headquarters :

1. The software technologies should be identified in consultation with the respective state government to ensure data transfer.
2. Since North East Region is a strategically located area, some of the data, especially security related information, needs to be protected. It is possible to use certain regulations and system to protect such data from being pilfered.
3. There may be a three-tier database: firstly, the information related to development, such as the necessary forms, information, policies of the NEC and the states of the region to be made available with a click of the mouse; secondly, the flow of communication between the DONER and the NEC, NEC and the respective state governments will be protected and only the concerned officials would be able to access it; and the third will be between the Secretary NEC, Chairman NEC, Members of the NEC, Secretaries to the Government of India and the Chief Secretaries of all eight states in the region. The decision to make database public will be prerogative of the members of this apex group.
4. The proposed hub will also provide video conferencing etc., if need be.

Focus on the First Database

While the second and the third database are for internal consumption of the NEC, but the real litmus test of the system will largely depend upon how efficiently the first data is updated, revised and made available to the people of this region. The following steps may help in achieving our goal:

1. *Language*: A customized easy communication language free from routine management jargons is a must for optimum utilization of the data. There is a need for regular evaluation of the data.

2. *Motivation*: It is generally experienced that IT-based transformation takes a lot of time. Therefore, patience is the key word for promoting business models for Community Information Centres.

3. *Channels*: Seldom we are able to consolidate and provide data from one window. Therefore a sector-wise database, which could also have sub-divisions for each geographical region should be developed. Since, it has already been suggested to evolve a three-tier database, there should not be any attempt to conceal data in the first channel.

4. *Defining Knowledge Source*: The knowledge source is defined in such a way to have a complementary role of evolving internal knowledge base to promote business and self employment. The product-process focus will help in marketing the NER products and help in improving and blending the traditional local products and knowledge on a hi-tech channel.

5. *Documentation Mode*: It is related to the systems whereby the organization stores knowledge.

6. *Evolution of Value Chain*: It will indicate in which areas of the value chain will help in skill development.

The P.P. Shrivastava Committee has already suggested the following measures:

(i) Comprehensive Computerisationa and efficient Management Information System (MIS) in the Secretariat, that makes daily reports of pending issues available and accessible to all to facilitate timely action and supervision at all times.

(ii) On-line maintenance of relevant databases, plans and projects, targets and evaluations, government circulars, especially relating to financial rules and procedural matters etc. for the information of officers, staff and the general public.

(iii) Training of all the officers and staff in computer-literacy and in modern management techniques.
(iv) Commissioning of reputed consultant(s) to work out systems and suggest time-bound action plan, so that the impact of NEC in its new statutory role is visible immediately.
(v) Orientation Motivational Courses highlighting the significance of NEC's functions so that the officers and staff take pride in their work and find it rewarding as well as means to self-improvement.

New Opportunities

The present IT centres in the country such as Bangalore and Gurgaon have saturated in the IT-related business. A large number of companies are looking for new destinations for setting up call centres and software parks. If the state governments take initiative, some of the top multinational companies such as Convergees, Dell and GE may set up centres in NER.

It is well-known that the Dell Company with a 5000-seat call centre was keen to have its huge set up in Lucknow, but due to the lethargic, bureaucratic approach of the local administration, Dell has shifted its operations to Chandigarh. Similarly, Convergees has shifted a few of its process to Philipenes. It also means that if we fail to tap these opportunities, some of the BPOs may shift their business outside India.

A few years ago, a call centre was set up in Guwahati. But it was closed due to certain reasons better known to the authorities. There is no dearth of human resource in this region. A large number of young men and women are presently employed in different BPOs in Bangalore, Gurgaon and Mumbai. It is an opportunity to lure some of the BPOs (Business Process Outsourcing) to the NER also. The employment generated from BPO will help in promoting harmony in the strife-torn society of this region.

The NEC may make renewed efforts to promote IT-based industry in the NER. The STPI (Software Technologies Parks in India) is already ready to make a little extra effort to promote IT-based industry in this region but it needs strong local initiative.

5

The Ground Situation

In the year 1991, India took a U-turn from the state sponsored economy based on the Industrial Policy Resolution (IPR) of 1956 to an open economy, where the state has to re-shift its key controls on economy and promotional role to a regulatory regime. It was not an easy task. The state controls on the economy had to be unshackled. The 1956 IPR had empowered the state to have its controls on the economy, especially in the core sectors. In the following years, the state was not only producing steel and power, but also pickles and juices and selling essential items like foodgrains. In this controlled economic regime, even the private sector expanded without much competition. The much appreciated mixed economy, which was based on the concept of the complementing roles of the government (public) sector and the private initiative. But it degenerated into a licence-quota raj. The huge investments, except few exceptions, were turned into redundant liabilities on the state and the people.

The processes of reforms and structural changes in our economic system were quietly and cautiously initiated by the then Finance Minister, Dr. Manmohan Singh, now our Prime Minister, in 1991. It was a very difficult task to usher in the economic reforms, when powerful vested interests were well-entrenched in our lethargic government machinery. In spite of opposition, the processes of reforms were initiated. It took almost more than a decade to really reverse the role of the state from the licence-quota raj to become a regulator for allowing level-playing role to private, initiative both national and international.

It is true that in certain sectors well-entrenched state sponsored players continue to resist this process even today, especially in the North Eastern States comprising all eight states. Due to various geographical and strategic factors, this region is still being liberally funded from the national funds. It is estimated that most of the financial requirements of the state budgets come from Union Budget. It has not really helped the people develop their own skill and take initiatives for evolving a self-sustained economy. Unemployment continues to haunt this region. A section of people might have been benefited, but for most of the people their very existence continues to be a harsh reality.

Before the 1991 reform process, a humble beginning of opening up and introduction of transparency in the economy had quietly been introduced during the mid-eighties of the last century. During Rajiv Gandhi's tenure as the Prime Minister, the then government successfully initiated information technology (IT) in the country. In spite of serious opposition, both in the political establishment and administration, concerted efforts were made to develop IT as an important tool of the governance and business. It is true that it took a few years for the country's political and business leadership to realize the potential of IT as the key tool for development and progress. After Rajiv Gandhi, successive prime ministers, irrespective of their political affiliations, promoted and continued IT in the country. These policies have led to India's leading position in this hi-tech sector in the world. But it is yet to percolate down for the benefit of masses. It must be appreciated that the Union Government has already taken definite steps for the promotion of IT in the North Eastern region. There is a need for creating awareness, especially in rural areas to introduce and popularize this hi-tech tool. It may take some time to reap the benefits of IT to various historical, geographical, social, economical and political reasons in this area.

The problem of the North Eastern region snowballed into a real economic and connectivity crisis following the partition of the country in 1947. Its natural business routes through East Bengal (now Bangladesh) were suddenly snapped. It may be noted that at the time of partition, it was not realized that the country's northeastern region would suddenly become a huge landlocked mass. The natural business routes of NER were suddenly choked due to the partition of the country.

The economy of this region has suffered. The partition of the country had transformed its traditional self-sustained economy into grant-led subsidized economic system. The natural business centres like Silchar, which was an important trading city of the undivided Assam (states like Nagaland, Arunachal, Meghalaya, Mizoram were once parts of Assam), is no more the business hub of this region. The further fragmentation of the undivided Assam into smaller states to cater to the local and regional aspirations has expanded the old simple bureaucratic set up into a vast network of government officials. It has made the common people economically cripple to be dependent upon only on the state-led initiatives for development and progress. There traditional tribal systems were also adversely affected.

With the signing of the regional cooperation agreement among the nations of this region, it appears cities like Silchar, which were once the hub of business in the North Eastern region, may regain their old glory. Their connectivity with the rest of India through long tortuous railway routes via north Bengal, sometimes through primitive meter gauge railway systems, may be replaced by opening of the borders with the neighbouring Bangladesh. The access to the Chittagong port, a natural port of business for this region, may boost the economy of this region. It has been an ordeal since the country's partition in 1947, to depend upon the Calcutta port, over a thousand kilometers from this hilly region.

All these physical, historical and administrative dimensions need to be closely studied and understood before a multi-pronged strategy could be effectively introduced to modernize its economic and business systems to unleash the hidden potential of this region.

Much of the present agony of this region is rooted to the partition and various conflicts witnessed in the past half-a-century. In spite of the not-so-friendly relations with the success governments in the neighbouring East Pakistan (now Bangladesh), the border trade continues, but through illegitimate channels. The ramifications of such trade arrangements have always been disastrous, both socially and politically. It is hoped that with the new regional groupings under the World Trade Organization (WTO), India and Bangladesh may have to find out ways and means to evolve a strong legitimate trade bindings, if they want to survive in the emerging competitive world trade, when even services will be open to the developed world.

It means each sector of human activity needs to be revamped, whether it is governance, banking, trade, education or medicare. In this new regime, the traditional government controls have to be removed and also the subsidy. The human resource is the key factor of the new emerging economic order. Fortunately, in education, the earlier initiatives are now paying rich dividends. A state like Mizoram has nearly 97 per cent literacy rate. In education, this state is almost at par with Kerala. However, in spite of the world-class human resources, the region is still backward in economic terms. It may be noted that in social consciousness and human behaviour, the North Eastern region is ahead of any part of the country. It only needs modern tools and the state-of-the-art strategies to tap its art natural resources and human potential.

Recognizing its remote geography, the country has always tried to support this region by providing additional resources in every field. The combined annual budget of all the eight North Eastern states comprising Assam, Arunachal, Manipur, Meghalaya, Mizoram, Nagaland, Sikkim and Tripura is nearly Rs. 26000 crores. Most of the support for this huge budget comes from the Union Government. Yet the impact of this huge investment is not commensurate with the funds being siphoned down in the various government or government-sponsored systems. Also, it appears the pro-active role of the Non-Governmental Organizations (NGOs) has also been diluted into a grant-receiving regime. Therefore, the challenge before us is how to make this region economically self-reliant and whether IT can play any role in unleashing the forces of economic growth in this sensitive region of the country.

6

The IT Initiative

More than two years have passed since the North East Business Summit was held on July 19-20 in 2002 in Mumbai, when the then IT Secretary in the Union Government, R.R. Shah, announced an ambitious roadmap for the penetration of IT in the region. It is only in this region of the country, where the Union Government has decided to set up Community Information Centre (CIC) project in all the 487 development blocks with V-sat connectivity. It may be noted that the V-sat technology being offered at the CICs provides broadband accessibility at 8 mbps to uplink with 128 kbps. It is much better than the dial-up protocol being made available to most of the people even in the cities like Mumbai, Delhi, Bangalore and Hyderabad.

Apart from normal E-mailing services, the CICs are expected to provide for a platform for E-Governance. It makes the North Eastern region better placed than the most of the country, as the IT platform will provide a continuous interface system between the government and common people.

This ambitious IT application programme in this region was further unfolded, when Mr. Shah explained that how would the CICs be playing a key-role in the local networking of schools, colleges and hospitals.

The IT ministry's plan to encourage use of the expansion of INTERNET through a technology called A22.11B, which will cover an area of four to five kilometers around the CICs. With the bandwidth of 128 kbph, rural markets, workshops will have easy access to the local as well as world markets. The concept of local action with global vision, popularly known as GVALA, becomes a reality. Dr. Kamal Taori, presently the NEC Secretary, has been promoting this GVALA concept for the past several years. During his innings in the Inter-State Council of Home Ministry and Planning

Commission, he campaigned for making IT as the backbone of entire planning process, administration and business. With the acceptance of making rural clusters for rural uplift and employment generation by the Planning Commission, Dr. Taori has tried to make it further operational by suggesting infusion of the pioneering work already done by Ashok Jhunjhunwala of IIT Chennai. It may be recalled that Jhunjhunwala received international acclaim for implementing an ambitious plan to provide NET connectivity in the deep dense rain forests of Amazon in South America. He is also trying to evolve a sustainable employment model in rural areas with IT support.

These CICs in NER were to become the keystone of development in the region. Even the educational institutions in the remote areas of this region should now have been experiencing the broadband connectivity. The doctors working in the local hospitals should have been consulting the specialists working even in far off places within India or abroad. Instead of making the CICs hub for communication for economic transactions, trade transactions, business transactions etc., they mostly give a deserted look these days. They function like government offices. They open only during office-hours. The CIC managers receive a salary, but no business incentive.

The vision of R.R. Shah of promoting the CICs as the nodal point of all rural activities is yet to take shape. He even had thought the CICs would not only educate, they would also provide the TV channels through the broadband connectivity to the local people. A series of community entertainment centres for masses will usher in an era of modern well-connected life for the people in remote areas. The feeling of isolation may soon end among the people of this region. With CICs provided with a video projector accompanied with a 29″ TV screen, the daylong business hub of the rural area could have been quietly turned into entertainment centre by evening. It is something, which the North Eastern region has got it, but the rest of India is yet to wait. But these is little effort to tap this opportunity.

7

Unique Opportunities on IT Platform

During the past five years or so, a large number of farmers in our country, mostly in the regions where they raise cash crops, have committed suicides due to indebtedness. Such incidents have mostly reported in the states like Maharashtra, Karnataka and Andhra Pradesh. But there are incidents, when the use of IT has not only saved the indebted depressed farmer from committing the extreme step, but has also brought prosperity to the farmer's family. In a recently published edition of a comptuer magazine, the success story of a farmer, Sandeep Tawde, has appeared, who had lost his poultry farm and was facing a total economic ruin. Tawde, 32, a Commerce Graduate, has set up a poultry farm at Baramati in Maharashtra. He went to a cyber cafe to locate new business opportunities for his products. He was able to get an on-line buyer from Taiwan to buy some of his products. Using IT as a tool, he has further expanded his business by getting some buyers even from Saudi Arabia.

The net result is that he is getting 60 per cent more profit from his newly discovered on-linc buyers. His success has enthused as many as 27000 farmers in the district, who too are getting themselves trained in the IT to be able to participate in this new IT-based market-driven economy.

If a Maharashtra farmer can turn around his sick unit and bring the much-needed prosperity for his nearly starving family, that too is possible in the North Eastern region. The possibility of opening up this close isolated geographical area has brightened up following the Kumming initiative. Kumming is the provincial capital of the Yunnan province of China. Yunnan is one of the most industrialized areas of Mainland China. The Kumming initiative is an attempt to evolve a cooperation regime among the close neighbours in the region, China, Myanmar, India and Bangladesh. This landlocked region comprising the North Eastern states, which has suffered the partition of the country in 1947, will now be able to be benefited by this regional agreement popularly called SAFTA (South Asian Free Trade Association). Another feature is that Myanmar has become member of the ASEAN, a common market of nearly 500 million prosperous people of South East Asia.

However, to reap benefits of the new opportunities, the people of the North Eastern Region have to be given level-playing ground in the free play of market forces. If adequate initiatives could not be taken within a specific time frame, it would only be a market for receiving imports from the better-developed economies of the neighbourhood. Therefore, for empowering people of this region, the policy makers have to evolve a twin strategy of encouraging the traditional handicrafts, agro-products and also modern industries. But it will only be possible by making the information technology the backbone of our business, trade and governance systems. Fortunately, the setting up of the Community Information Centres (CICs) at block level is a very good beginning. Some people feel that the CICs are not being used in the countryside. Except a few CICs in Assam, most of them are suffering losses. However, by adopting correct strategies, it is possible to make these CICs into small business hub even in the remote countryside of the North Eastern states.

The Beginning

It is a fact that despite pumping billions of rupees in the North Eastern states collected from various taxes from the common people of the country, the economic growth of this region could not take off. It has dismayed most of the policy makers, who feel that the investment in the region is becoming counter-productive. The conflict situation has also further discouraged those who believe that this region will soon become an economic powerhouse. There could be many reasons for this not-too-encouraging performance, but it is also a fact that the people of these states are very hard working and the incidents of violence continue to adversely affect their economic growth.

It needs a lot of explaining that despite availability of funds, the process of e-governance could not take pace in the region. Except Tripura, where the state government has taken definite steps towards e-governance, most of the state administrations are yet to be geared up for introducing e-governance in their respective areas. It is true that even in the so-called IT-advanced states like Karnataka and Andhra Pradesh, the process of the e-governance is yet to take off at the grassroots level.

It is a signal for an imminent disaster for any society, when its large number of young men and women suffer unemployment and the culture of violence creeps into the system. It is a vicious circle. Hardly any economic prosperity can come under the shadow of guns, and it is also true without generating hope and employment opportunity the violence cannot end.

Cluster—The Hope Model

While the Planning Commission was formulating the 10th Plan document, a Task Force on Employment Strategies and Employment Monitoring was set up under the chairmanship of Dr. S.P. Gupta, a noted economist and then one of the members of the Planning Commission. It suggested an ambitious programme of generating ten million employment opportunities per year during the Tenth Plan period. Of this, 9.26 million is proposed to be from primary sector, 14.48 million from secondary sector and 25.26 million from the tertiary sector. Of the secondary sector, it is proposed to generate 10.14 million jobs through programme-based activities like Khadi Village and Industries Commission (KVIC) and other small and tiny sectors.

A committee under the chairmanship of Vijay Mahajan, nearly 10 years ago in 1994, suggested various measures of encouraging investment opportunities in the rural areas. It also discussed the constraints and potential for evolving suitable strategies in this vital sector. The Swiss Development Corporation and the National Bank for Agriculture and Rural Development (NABARD) jointly funded it. It grouped some of the areas into emergent sub-sectors, high growth sub-sectors and high share sub-sectors. In the emergent sub-sectors, it identified agro services and rural transport in Assam. It also concluded that rural, small and micro enterprise sector in the country has a promise of becoming the most dynamic part of economy, both rural and urban. It has the possibility to absorb as many as 45 million new entrants to the employment market out of nearly 100 million who would be seeking employment opportuniteis in the next decade.

It is true NABARD as an apex bank in this sector has taken a number of initiatives. In its efforts to refinance the rural non-farm sector (RNFS), it has funded over Rs. 9100 crores and helped in creating job opportunities for 60 lakh people. Apart from RNFS, it has also directly helped NGOs/voluntary agencies/other developmental agencies in experimenting with various activities supporting this non-farm sector. It included a number of promotional programmes. However, the optimum benefits of these programmes could not really benefit the poor due to various factors. In most of the NABARD sponsored clusters, its members were already defaulters and could not get finance for their projects. Although the NABARD has tried to resolve this problem by constituting self-help groups, the impact of such clusters could not really benefit the villagers. Maybe, it will be advisable to try Dr. Kamal Taori's strategy. It is popularly known as the Taorian Model of Rural Empowerment, which envisages a convergence of all the resources available and use of information technology as the basic platform for all possible activities.

It was decided at the NEC (North Eastern Council) meeting held on 30 October, 2004 to take appropriate steps for optimum capacity utilization of existing resources in all sectors, including IT in the region for faster economic growth and employment generation. It was envisaged to create Rural Entrepreneur Development Convergence Centres at an investment to the tune of Rs. 800 crores for 400-odd blocks of 80 or so districts in all the North Eastern states. The role of the IT will be of an effective tool for two-way flow of information/directions, for effective real-time monitoring of various ongoing projects, promotion of business and trade, and for dissemination of information as a means of public-private partnership with a view to seeking their involvement, cooperation, participation, and ensuring transparency.

These widely dispersed centres would have to be interlinked with IT network for communication and dissemination of information for promoting rural industry, local initiatives and employment generation. Thus CICs become the backbone of new rural economy.

The Recommendations

A number of issues related to IT were discussed in the two-day brain storming session (September 29-30) on **Mission IT** for **Masses,** held at the Indian Institute of Entrepreneurship. H.E. Governor of Assam, Lt. General (retd.) Ajai Singh, inaugurated the seminar, which was attended by some of the leading players in the IT industry such as Microsoft and the well-known public sector undertaking, Software Technology Parks of India Ltd. (STPI). There was near unanimity that with the setting up of CICs in the region it is possible to penetrate IT in the remote areas of this region. Even the people living in such difficult areas now can avail the benefits of IT. Some of the leading players in this sector offered help in promoting IT in the region.

The following measures were suggested for evolving a strategy and a definite roadmap on IT-led development process, which may revolutionize the current level of planning and perception of economic progress in the region:

1. A user-friendly IT programme teaching the basics of computer use and Internet may immediately be initiated through well-known institutions.
2. Referring to the non-utilization or low-capacity utilization of the CICs, it was suggested that there should be an effective campaign among villages to utilize this hi-tech facility.
3. It was suggested that a net-based specific area customized rural and agricultural extension programme should be introduced with an active on-line connectivity with nearest veterinary doctors, hospitals, agriculture universities and colleges.
4. There is an urgent need for public-private partnership in this crucial area to encourage private initiative in popularizing the IT-based services.
5. The various government schemes in this region in the three key areas G-to-G (Government to Government), G-to-B (Government to Business) and G-to-C (Government to

Citizen) need to be implemented on a war footing for immediate results for making e-governance a reality in the region.

6. The NEC should approach all the eight state governments to immediately introduce these schemes, as large funds received from the IT Ministry of the Union Government are yet to be fully utilized by them.
7. For a serious beginning in this sensitive sector, the NEC must evolve its own hub and provide all necessary information to citizens on its website.
8. For better coordination, the NEC may approach the state governments for seeking details about the IT-related help such as providing comptuers etc. to various educational institutions for launching awareness and IT-literacy programme in the region.
9. All development projects should make IT as the backbone of disseminating information and its faster development.
10. The NEC being a nodal agency may constitute a task force comprising all IT secretaries in various state governments in the region for a uniform approach in evolving IT-related information platforms and archives for better interaction.
11. In the proposed committee of the IT Secreataries, NEC may also request representatives of various organizations active in the IT sector.

The Road Ahead

There is a saying that if we do not practise ourselves, we cannot really preach. It is true about NEC too. The NEC should immediately try to set up an IT hub to have an on-line connectivity with all the state secretariats in the region and its website should be on a user-friendly platform.

Dr. Arun Kumar Verma, former director, Science and Technology of NEC, has already done the necessary groundwork in this context. He has already introduced intelligent character recognition system in one of universities of the region, Manipur and five school boards of education in different states. As many as 700 schools have already been covered in the NEC sponsored IT education programme. It included teachers' IT familiarization programme.

There is an urgent need for dedicated communication network as suggested by ITDGNE (Information Technology Development Group for North East region) held on 17th August, 2001 at NEC, Shillong.

Initially, this programme was to be limited to IT education and for opening of computer syllabus in schools. However, following an impact analysis, it was observed, some of the schools successfully generated income and employment by appointing teachers. This has happened in case of colleges too. There is a need to promote such activities to make even these school computer centres self-sufficient and economically viable.

In Tura area in Meghalaya, St. Xavier's School having the comptuers adopted a few rural schools in the nearby villages during the winter holidays to impart computer training without charging any fee. It also helped them identify talent for IT. Similarly, in Nagaland, the Vision School, Dimapur, took initiative in holding IT-familiarization seminar with the local people. Out of these schools supported by NEC, nine have received President's Excellence Award.

Some districts like the Jorhat district office has already set up G-to-C information platform for the citizens of the district to get the information with a push of a button or by paying a small fee at the various government offices in the district.

The Assam government has recently signed an agreement with the Power Grid Corporation of India, a public sector undertaking, to allow "way to passage" for IT connectivity in the state. It means that IT connectivity will soon be spreading through the electricity lines to a common household. The NEC may coordinate such agreements with other states and the Power Grid Corporation of India.

The decisions taken regarding a holistic concept of development at the NEC Secretariat meeting on October 30, 2004, presided over by the NEC Chairman and Governor of Assam, Lt. General (retd.) Ajai Singh, cannot really take off the ground unless the optimal capacity utilization of the existing IT network could not be put to use.

The strategy for creating Rural Entrepreneurship

Development Convergence Centres, which has an initial programme to raise a sum of Rs. 800 crores for 400 development blocks of 80 or so districts in the North Eastern region requires cluster development around CICs. The funding for this ambitious project may be raised through various banks such as NABARD, SIDBI and other leasing companies. It is possible to seek investment of Rs. two crores in each block with a small NEC seed money.

The NEC has already floated a global tender for buying computers and software for various educational institutions. It is high time that the efforts already made in this sector should be implemented without any further delay.

The NEC may contact the Rail Tel, the Railway Ministry-sponsored public sector undertaking, which has laid Optical Fibre Network (OFN) connecting 7000 railway stations in the country. The Rail Tel may set up Cyber Cafes or hi-tech cities in this region, mostly in Assam, for promoting industry, education, trade and business. Such centres may be set up near markets, commercial centres and those railway stations, where freight movement is allowed.

The concept of public-private partnership in the IT sector may give a new thrust to an all round development in the region, if in its various committees, especially in the field of IT, NEC may involve CII (Local branch), North Eastern Chambers of Commerce (NECC), universities, schools and colleges, and other NGOs.

8

North Eastern Council Initiative

During the first meeting of the Information Technology Development Group of NE region (ITDGNE) held on 17 August, 2000, a number of steps were taken for promoting computer education in the NER. The participants agreed that there is a need for intensive computer education. The importance of working out the 10th Five Year Plan and long-term perspective plan keeping in mind the status of the infrastructure available in the region to develop IT manpower linked with other IT infrastructure like NE IT park and communication centres.

Dr. A.K. Verma, the then Director (Science & Technology) and Member Secretary, ITDGNE, in his detalied presentation explained about the guidelines of the ITDGNE, available IT education infrastructure, existing national scenario of IT and electronics, present telecom infrastructure of NE region and tele-density compared with national level and its comparison with other countries, potential of the IT enabled services, e-commerce and e-governance, IT-citizen interface, existing IT infrastructure of the NE region and projected different programmes and plan to develop the region in the field of IT, which has been recognized by the Union Government as a dynamic vehicle to transform the present slow growth to rapid development of the economy.

1. IT Education Programme for North Eastern Region

During the presentation, effort of NEC for covering 305 secondary and higher secondary schools of NE region, which started during 1994-95, for providing the secondary and higher secondary level computer education was appreciated by all members. Under this scheme, apart from computer and other peripheral, NEC is providing specialized training programmes to computer teachers for six-month duration.

1.1. Computer School Education Programme

There are more than 5500 secondary/higher secondary schools in the NE region. Of these schools NEC has already provided computer infrastructure and other related assistance, including dedicated computer training to school teachers, to as many as 305 schools. In each institution one computer training centre was established. During the 10th five year plan, the committee has recommended to cover 1000 schools under this programme as a part of national goal to provide computer education in all schools by 2008.

1.2 Higher Programmes on IT: [MCA, M.Sc. (CS), BCA, B.Sc. (CS), Master of Information Technology, PGDCA]

The existing infrastructure of the NE states having these courses was discussed in detail. During the discussion, it was found that there are only three institutes (Tezpur University, Jorhat Engineering College, and a private institution at Guwahati) conducting MCA course (intake : 120) and Guwahati University [M.Sc.(CS)] and Tezpur University (Master of IT), in addition to one/two institutions-like St. Anthony's College, Shillong: (PGDCA) in the region. There are many universities, which are not involved in computer education programmes like MCA, M.Sc (CS) or M.Sc (IT) courses. It was also felt during the meeting that the existing engineering colleges may also join the venture of starting any of the above courses or double their intake capacity after creating adequate infrastructure. It was decided during the meeting that unless NE region was able to create proper infrastructure for computer education at different levels, it might not be possible to bring IT industry/IT software development in the region. It is also felt during the meeting that IT education at different levels is the urgent need of the region and a proper strategy in this direction is a must starting from high-end level of IT software developemnt work to lower-end level of IT enabled services/ services/IT Citizen Services/E-Commerce, where diploma/BCA/

PGDCA may be able to cater to the needs of the region/nation in the IT global environment. The existing colleges (degree level) may start the lower level programme [BCA, PGDCA, B.Sc.(CS)] in order to create the manpower for selection to higher level computer education [M.Sc.(CS), MCA, MIT] in the university/institute and also to join the IT-enabled services and other IT-related emerging activities.

1.2.1 For University/Engineering College Institute

For starting M.Sc. (CS), MCA, MIT courses: (a) Ten universities of NE states may start M.Sc (CS)/MCA courses with intake capacity of 30, and (b) Four existing engineering colleges may start MCA course with 30 intake capacity each under self financing scheme for running the courses. The existing university/institutes already running MCA course would be encouraged to double their intake capacity.

1.2.2 For Colleges: to start B.Sc(CS), BCA and PGDCA courses

There are more than 300 degree level colleges in the north eastern region, where different computer courses can be started as mentioned above in order to generate manpower of diploma level for joining IT-enabled services and also undertaking higher education [M.Sc(CS), MCA courses]. The modalities of this scheme are the same as M.Sc (CS)/MCA courses under self-financing scheme.

1.3 Sponsoring of Students for M.Tech (Electronics & IT subject) for generating common pool of faculty resource

The current problem of quality faculty in the computer science/ engineering was discussed in detail which is due to current trend of shifting competent faculty into the IT industry as a result of higher salary and carrier growth. Members were of the opinion that due to the present trend of growth in IT industry, it has become difficult to retain qualified manpower in the present salary structure. It was also agreed to offer a proper incentive to attract faculty to the educational institutions. It was also decided that NEC may evolve a strategy for sponsoring students for M. Tech course (Computer & IT) in the reputed institutes for students studying in the existing institutes of NE states. An agreement to be signed between NEC and the sponsored institute that the candidate has to serve a minimum period of five years in the particular institute after completion of M. Tech course. In this way, qualified manpower will be available as a faculty to the different institutions of NE region. It has been decided that NEC may evolve this mechanism from the reputed institutions like IIT for getting seats and other modalities.

1.4 IT education for computer and electronics in the existing engineering colleges and polytechnics

The members were apprised of that a Project "IMPACT (Industrially oriented manpower with appropriate competence and training) for NE region." They were told that this project is under consideration as a joint programme between NEC and Ministry of Information Technology for electronics and computer science department of the existing engineering colleges and polytechnics of the NE region. Its main purpose is to strengthen computer and electronics infrastructure, V-sat based internet connectivity, faculty training programmes and industry interface training to students so that competent manpower may be developed.

1.5 Setting up of North Eastern Regional Institute of Information Technology (NERIIT)

The interim report of the task force on HRD in IT has recommended for setting up of "Institute of Information Technology" which can function as a resource institution at the regional/state level. IT task force also recommended for setting up of five IIITs, out of which, two IIITs have been set up by the Government of India. International Institute of Information Technology at Hyderabad has been established by the Andhra Pradesh State Government in collaboration with IT industry. The interim report has also mentioned that an exclusive institute of IT may be established with state/central funding (and possibly external funding) and industry collaboration. The institute would offer training in cutting edge technology in addition to offering bridge courses.

2.0 Intelligent Character Recognition System for Secondary/ Higher Secondary Board of NE Region

ICR system is basically to eliminate manual data entry and based on automatic scanning of forms with high speed image capture, batch scanning, character recognition and conversion into ASCII characters, verifications and correction, validation of data scanned in order to prepare admit card, marks-sheet, result card, certificate, etc. which also eliminates the manipulations due to this system.

Based on the proposal of the government of Manipur for this system for Board of Secondary Education, ICR system with all peripheral support such as PC, Printer, Scanner, Heavy duty laser printer and training to the Board officials is being designed. The ICR system for the Board of Secondary Education for all NE states needs to be installed.

3.0 Tele-Medicine Network for North Eastern Region

The tele-medicine network is being designed by the DECU (Development and Educational Communication Unit) office, Department of Space, Ahemedabad, for connecting the RIMS, three medical colleges of Assam with all district hospitals. During the discussion, it was also decided to connect Bangalore-based Apollo Hospital and Kolkata-based Asia Heart Foundation with the medical institutions of NE states for super specialization consultancy.

4.0 V-SAT-Based Secure Communication Network for North Eastern Region

This network is basically for state functionary of the NE states including NEC by connecting state headquarters, district headquarters and block headquarters under closed user group having message security on voice and data communication. The potential users of the network were discussed in detail and a number of probable users at different levels of sites. This network is different from pol-net due to its different type of utilization by the state functionary and NEC. This network is being designed by Space Applications Centre, Ahmedabad. This was discussed in detail by members.

5.0 Information Technology Infrastructure of IT industry (IT Park, High Speed Broad-band communication network, IT Software Development firm and IT enabled services; and IT policy and Incentives by State Government)

During the meeting information technology infrastructure in NE was discussed in detail, especially the main requirement to IT industry in the region. Software Technology Park, Information Technology Park are basically 100 per cent EOU for undertaking software development work using the high speed data communication link—for physical export (electronics and software) of professional services—or consultancy services/development of software. This can be set up by the Central Government/State Government/PSU or any combinations. During the discussion, initiatives of Andhra Pradesh in this regard were highlighted, which NE region is required to follow, including the facilities available at HITEC and STPI, if IT industry is desired to be developed. The state governments in NER were requested to work out and finalize IT policy and fiscal incentives to attract the MNCs for setting up of their centre once the basic infrastructure are created. The restriction imposed by different states of NER, may not be conducive to develop IT export potential and IT based economy in the region. During the meeting, it was decided that NER may act as main hub for IT export zone to South East Asian nations. Its very close proximity to these countries may help IT as a main source to develop the economy in the region. However, a proper IT infrastructure and State IT policy and effort by the state governments are important factors for achieving the target. It was also decided that regional level IT zone may be developed at Shillong, which may be interfaced with state-level IT park for providing the high speed broadband communication network for international business operations, different direct carriers to different countries, Internet services on the pattern of the Hyderabad. IT incentive policies for IT software development firms and IT enabled services, including e-governance may be evolved by the state governments.

5.1 Setting up of Regional Level Information Technology Development Park for NE region at Shillong interfaced with

State level IT Park: This should consist of all facilities required for IT activities which can act as a main hub for IT export zone for South East Asian countries.

5.2 Dedicated broadband communication Network for NE region for data communication network for internet connectivity: Cost to be worked out.

5.3 State governments are requested to finalize IT policy to bring EOU IT firms in the region.

5.4 The different restrictions (such as Inner-line permit) imposed by the state governments may not be conducive for the growth of IT in the region.

5.5 IT enabled services (Call Centres, Medical Transcriptions, Back office processing, IT services for e-governance) to be encouraged in addition to IT industry.

6.0 North Eastern Space Applications Centre (NESAC)

Total expenditure for a five-year programme for establishing infrastructure is Rs. 40.0 crores which are required to be borne by NEC and DOS (Department of Science) on 50:50 sharing basis. Hence, Rs. 20.0 crores may be earmarked for this centre for the 10th Five Year Plan. Similarly, tentative expenditure for establishing the development communication network and remote sensing application work have been projected.

9

A Security Perspective

Apart from its key-role in the planning and fomulating policies for faster economic growth in this sensitive region, the North Eastern Council has also been given a crucial role in the security concerns of the eight states of the northeast region (NER). Since the information technology (IT) has become central to the way the governments, business and social movements organize themselves, the terrorists and criminals too are increasingly using IT for achieving their regional and global objectives. It is now a well-known fact that with the growing penetration of the information communication technologies (ICTs) penetrating various conflict zones in the world, the dark forces of violence too have access to this modern tool.

It is true that our knowledge so far about the degree of penetration of these technologies in the conflict zones is yet to be assessed, but the military actors, whether they represent state or militants, consider ICT infrastructure as a potential war-waging tool to humble their respective adversaries. This tool can empower new actors and open up new terrain of battlefields. On the other hand, those who believe ICT infrastructure as a "neutral" continue to promote it as an agent of change. The answer, perhaps, is that the instruments of state should use these dual-purpose hi-tech tools for development as well as for keeping a close vigil on security dimensions in a respective area.

With the emergence of Internet and IT in human activities, the traditional geographical boundaries are increasingly becoming irrelevant. Therefore, there is an urgent need that our traditional concepts—from privacy to surveillance, vulnerability and above all, security aspects, should be revised and updated in the current digital environment. In the post-9/11 era, the security concerns have received a total new approach. The security agencies world over are closely examining the relationship between IT and security. Scholars from various disciplines too are engaged in exploring the new nature of IT-related threats, the new power structures emerging around ICT. Also, the ethical and political implications arising from this complex and important field concerning the entire human race.

The Ignorance

The consequences and potential manifestation of the IT, which in general parlance is called *cyber-aggression,* are yet to be fully articulated and understood. In case of NER, a thorough study of its various dimensions needs to be undertaken. A proper classification of the security threats in its diversified environs is required. It is not a case of ordinary policing, but a complex scenario in this upcoming region, which is adjacent to not-so-friendly neighbours. Although due to growing worldwide opposition to terrorism, it appears that peace may soon knock in this turbulent region too. But new security challenges may appear in the new environment, especailly when the traditional known violent activities of certain militants and terrorist groups are quietly becoming hi-tech.

It is true that there is some realization among the policy makers about the ICT's role in the security, but there is a need to create full awareness and implications about cyber aggression and its manifestation. There is a need for a continuous understanding and revision of the nature of the problem and also what strategies need to be evolved and adopted to counter such aggressions.

It has been our experience that on many occasions militants and terrorists are better equipped than our security forces. Therefore, it is high time that our progress in the civil use of IT should be accompanied with adequate cyber-security measures. At present, most of the cyber-security measures evolve around protection of critical IT-related infrastructure in the private sector. There is a need to adopt measures in the form enhanced security software, incident reporting and information sharing among the various agencies.

It is the high time that NEC assumes a coordinating role by incorporating various security agencies and software experts from institutions like IITs. It may also consider setting up an infromal core group comprising chiefs of security agencies from the state governments and central government to understand the subtle nuances of the cyber threats. The NEC initiative may help in pro-active strategic measures before a catastrophic situation hits the region. A beginning may be made by involving both academic and security institutions to sensitize themselves to the problems related to the cyber-threats. A care is to be taken that this initiative does not become a routine affair and be a prisoner of bureaucratic jungle. As soon as dimensions and potentials of the cyber-related threats are clear, each player may be allowed to have its own evolutionary processes. They will be working separately but not in isolation. The networking will ensure the much needed coordination among them.

The Big Brother Watches the World

The IT recommendations will remain incomplete without discussing the ECHLEON system, the global communications interception system jointly run by USA-UK alliance comprising United States of America, United Kingdom, Canada, Australia and New Zealand. With this system, it is possible for the USA to monitor and retrieve any information by using the supercomputers installed under the ECHLEON system. Similarly, Russia and China too have been trying to evolve and install such systems in their respective countries.

It is believed to be very costly for developing such monitoring systems. But with an innovative systematic approach, a strong database can be created to provide a strong information system for security agencies. Earlier, the decryption agencies were largely hidden from public view. But with IT, information on surveillance is more under public scrutiny. At the same time, IT provides availability of much more communication intelligence for surveillance. The storage cost has also been considerably reduced due to the new technological innovations.

The Advice

The challenges in cyberspace are basically focused to prevent three main threats—damage to comptuer system, corruption or destruction of the contained information and leakage of sensitive information to the adversaries. Similarly, mischief may be classified into those who perpetuate directly (such as hackers) and those who intervene indirectly using bad codes to soften the site they plan to hit.

Therefore, the following cautious approach may be adopted:

1. A system of continous processing has to be evolved for IT-related issues to tackle cyber-related crimes seriously. They have to be and they are analyzed in the framework of the prevailing overall security perspective in the region. It may be noted that in most of cases we may not be able to ascertain immediately the conspirators. It will help us monitor and if need be throw out the mischief mongers before they succeed in engineering any violence.
2. The NEC hub may evolve a system of maintaining data of thousands of people who visit this region. Even with a little effort, we may have details about the penetration of Bangladeshis in the Indian side. It may help the security agencies, which may be able to update their information on a continuous basis. It will be an important tool for surveillance and, to some extent, will help in resolving the problem of identifying the troublemakers.
3. The NEC's key role in the security of the region will receive general appreciation as its security related IT-based initiatives would end the current mismatch between the border controls and internal surveillance systems.
4. As a democratic country, we cannot really monitor the inland travellers, but most of the passengers travel by buses, trains and civil aircrafts, which can be recorded without violating any privacy of our citizens. Even the records of the inner-line permits will be quite useful to our security agencies.
5. Since the NEC hub may have a lot of security-related data, it is necessary to adopt cautious approach before selecting any software company to provide the hub and its maintenance.

PART II

E-GOVERNANCE

10

The NASSCOM Report

This document will remain incomplete, if the executive summary of the NASSCOM (National Association of Software and Service Companies) report is not incorporated. Although this report is yet to be critically evaluated, it offers an insight into various dimensions of this sector. As usual such reports begin with high optimism, but it has raised certain policy issues and also lack of the government initiatives in certain key sectors. It may be noted that the NER is also suffering due to lack of awareness of the government machinery at subordinate level.

The executive summary is being presented in this document to help the policy makers and software experts and promoters evolve a better strategy to promote this sector in the NER.

Major Findings

India's information technology (IT) prowess is unquestionable. The software and services sectors have transformed India into a global high-tech leader. It is commonly agreed that three factors account for India's success: the creativity, hard work, and dedication of workforce; high levels of education and English proficiency; and, most important, *government policy that promotes free enterprise and allows the IT sector to flouish.*

However, a strategy that focuses on export markets might have come at the expense of IT uptake in the domestic market. Indeed, the results of this study suggest that *India is underinvested in IT capital. IT capital that does exist in India is not widely dispersed and significant work remains to extend the benefits of IT throughout India's economy.*

We believe that government policy focusing on *promotion of*

IT capital deepening in IT-using segments of the economy (businesses, households, educational institutions, and the government itself), especially software asset deepening, will generate and disperse more widely the benefits of IT throughout India.

Drawing on the experiences of India's commercially successful IT export sector, evaluating successful IT markets worldwide, and surveying policy influentials within India, we believe the *following policy areas will be key to IT capital deepening in India's positive government enablement, human capital, intellectual property protection, infrastructure development, research and development, and trade and tax policy.*

Specific Findings: IT and the Economy of India

India's economy is underinvested in IT capital. Among 30 economies worldwide, its IT capital share that separates invested from underinvested economies is 10 per cent. The IT capital share in India's economy—only 3.5 per cent of total capital—is lowest among all economies considered.

Dispersion of existing IT capital in India's economy is narrower than in any of the 30 economies examined. The Personal Computer (PC) penetration rate in India is less than 12 per cent of the average rate in other economies underinvested in IT capital. The Internet penetration rate in India is less than 16 per cent of the average rate in other economies underinvested in IT capital. The penetration rate of secure Internet servers in India is less than 6 per cent of the average rate in underinvested economies.

As a result of being underinvested in IT capital, economic growth and productivity are low in India. Gross Domestic Product (GDP) per hour worked in India is less than three-fourths of the average rate in all economies underinvested in IT capital.

Three major factors explain why India's economy is underinvested in IT capital. First, India's economy is poor. In our survey, annual per capita GDP in India is less than two-thirds of the average in the next poorest economy underinvested in IT capital (the Philippines). Second, despite recent trade liberalization, import tariffs and taxes remain in effect on IT hardware. These tariffs increase the price of hardware and software, thereby reducing investment spending on IT capital. Third, like all governments, the Indian government is a major source of demand for IT products and services. However, the Indian government's IT procurement policies and practices are neither competitive nor transparent, discouraging vendors from entering the market.

Until there is IT capital deepening in India, the economy will not benefit fully from annual investments in IT. In economies invested in IT capital, a 10 per cent increase in IT capital increases GDP 3.6 per cent; a 10 per cent increase in labour hours increases GDP 4 per cent. In contrast, in economies underinvested in IT capital, a 10 per cent increase in IT capital increases GDP only 1.6 per cent. As IT capital deepens in an economy, IT capital adds more to GDP and, more important, labour becomes more productive.

Specific Findings: The Policy Prescription

For India's economy to become invested in IT capital, the government must develop and implement policies that promote investment in IT by businesses, households, educational institutions, and the government itself.

Policies should focus on promotion of software asset investment in India. Relative to all other economies examined, annual domestic investment in software assets as a share of total domestic IT investment is lowest in India.

Seven policy areas will be key to IT capital deepening in India.

Positive government enablement

- Policy influentials surveyed agreed most strongly with the statement, "Positive government engagement, not protectionism, is important to fostering the domestic IT market." The rank score of this statement was 4.9 out of a possible 5. A score of 1 indicates strong disagreement and a score of 5 indicates strong agreement.
- India's economy is advantaged by the government's decision to allow the market to drive technological development of the IT sector and software industry.

Trade and tax policy

- Tax lesson from the success of software and IT services industries serving foreign markets should be applied to industries serving the domestic market.
- India maintains some of the highest taxes on computers worldwide, nearly 19 per cent. These taxes raise the price of IT and dampen IT investment. The effects can be seen in low PC and Internet penetration rates in India.
- Most policy influentials surveyed agree strongly with the statements, "Liberal tax policy is important to fostering the domestic IT industry" (rank score of 4.7) and "The government should eliminate taxes on IT products" (rank score of 4.3).

Access to finance capital for domestically focused IT companies

- Overall, capital might not be as readily available in India as some officials believe.
- A Milken Institute Survey ranks India at 41 out of 51 countries in terms of capital availability. China ranks 33.
- According to the World Bank statistics, foreign direct investment (FDI) accounts for 85.4 per cent of gross capital formation in Ireland. By comparison, FDI accounts for only 2.1 per cent of gross capital formation in India.
- When asked to agree or disagree with the statement, "Venture capital is generally available," respondents gave it a rank scrore of 2.6.
- In some cases, there was a slight difference between government influentials' and private sector's opinion on the situation, which suggests a need for further discussion and communication.

Research and development

- While respondents generally agree that research and development (R&D) is important in fostering a domestic IT industry (rank score of 4.7), most respondents believe that the elements for a successful R&D policy in India are absent.

- Research in India, as manifested by articles published in technical journals, lags behind China. In 1999, China published over 11,000 technical journal articles; India published 9,000.
- Development and commercialization of new technologies in India lags behind China. In 2002, India received $12 million in licenses and royalty receipts. China received more than 15 times that amount, $133 million, in the same year.
- Despite this relatively poor performance, cluster development in India—one of the keys to R&D success—is higher in India than in China and many other countries.
- This conflicting information suggests more needs to be done to target R&D to India's domestic market needs.

Intellectual property protection

- The software piracy rate in India is (73 per cent) high. The average rate in the Asia Pacific region (53 per cent) is one-third lower than India's.
- A study by the National Bureau of Economic Research (NBER) finds that regulatory quality, including effective property protection, is a statistically significant factor explaining PC and Internet penetration rates. Hence, India's high software piracy rate helps explain the low PC and Internet penetration rates in India's economy.
- In addition, previous analysis by Nathan Associates Inc. and Sallstrom Consulting found a strong correlation between intellectual property protection and economic growth. A 10 per cent decrease in software piracy rates is associated with a 13.4 per cent increase in GDP. Hence, India's high software piracy rate may help explain the economy's low GDP per capita and slow rate of IT uptake.
- Many of the policy influentials surveyed believe intellectual property protection is important for domestic IT growth, but few understand the significance of various treaties and obligations.
- The most significant missing policy element in the area of intellectual property protection is enforcement of existing laws.

Human capital

- India has some of the best engineers and computer programmers worldwide, but policy influentials believe the quality of the economy's engineers varies from state to state.
- India's IT talent is not adequately focused on the domestic market.
- The domestic market needs to be better prepared to use IT. The acquisition of IT skills should be promoted through broader education in basic literacy, greater use of computers in schools, and greater access to computers throughout the country.

Physical IT and communications infrastructure

- Of all the policies examined, policy influentials were most concerned about the state of the IT and communications infrastructure in India.
- Nearly everyone surveyed strongly agreed the "Strong telecommunications and Internet infrastructure is important to growing the local IT market," assigning it a rank score of 4.9.
- Of most concern is broadband deployment and Internet use. No other statements were disagreed with more strongly than the statements regarding the adequacy of broadband deployment and Internet use:
  - —When presented with the statement "Broadband is sufficiently deployed in India," respondents disagreed strongly, assigning it a rank score of 1.2.
  - —When presented with the statement, "Internet usage in India is adequate", respondents disagreed strongly, assigning it a rank score of 1.5.
  - —When presented with the statement "The government has done enough to provide access to Internet infrastructure," respondents disagreed strongly, assigning it a rank scrore of 1.6.

11

Dr. Kamal Taori's Perspective of E-Governance

The developing countries including India suffer mostly because seldom are they able to strongly challenge the growing economic hegemony of the developed world comprising USA and the European Union. It may be recalled that they had agreed during the Doha round of discussions in the WTO (World Trade Organisation) that farm subsidy should be reduced, but now they insist that developing countries should reduce the subsidy in agricultural inputs to their small and medium farmers. But they want to continue their huge subsidies believed to be to the tune of US $50 billion annually to their farmers. It may be noted that only 5–7 per cent of the population in the developed world is dependent on agriculture, while more than 75 per cent of our population continues to be dependent upon agriculture, which continues to faces the vagaries of nature.

There are two aspects of the WTO's march into the rural economy. The protected sector will now be open to the world's financial high and low tides. While entire financial systems are under the control of multinational financial institutions dominated by the world's most prosperous countries, they may able to sustain these financial fluctuations but to expect poor Indian farmers, mostly living in rural areas, to sustain and survive in this new economic world order will nearly herald an end to their small but self-sustaining economy.

E-Governance

Information technology is an effective tool that can bridge the vast communication gap in rural areas. It is possible now to blend development strategy with a global vision and local action (GVALA). If the entire delivery system for rural uplift and networking could be transferred to computer networks, it would be possible to provide global access to rural products.

This essay ventures to find out the missing links with reference to definitions, clarity, brevity and issues related to faster growth with special reference to globalisation, and challenges of our time, when the country's close economy regime is quietly opening up to global pressures and challenges. Needless to say, unless these basic problems of clarity in definitions and a holistic approach without missing any dimension are fully attended and understood, any amount of discussion, analysis or plan of action will not really trigger off the forces of development in the countryside. Our experience of planning processes introduced since our independence, despite some spectacular achievements, does not inspire hope or optimism. The current model of development has caused despair even among the planners. Ask any authority, the reply would be an affirmation of a hopeless situation. It is here that the subject of holistic development must be taken seriously, which may give a new hope of a win-win situation for all of us. But it requires transparency, it has to be paramount both at policy level and its implementation in the field.

Defining Old Concepts Afresh

Our policy makers have become prisoners of some traditional phrases such as exploiters and exploited, urban or rural, organised or unorganised, literate or illiterate, men or women, south or north, etc. Therefore, we have to focus and identify the people whom we really want to address. If we draw a whole picture or adopt a holistic approach, we may find that there are many dimensions of India, which have never been looked into with a holistic approach and continue to be ignored even at the policy level.

We should realise that the firm stand taken by Commerce Minister Arun Jaitley (now by Kamal Nath) needs to be fully supported by a strong strategy with a devoted team of people engaged in giving a push to the rural economy. This innovative approach cannot be really implemented at the ground level unless we also reform our approach and strategies of the policy levels at the central government as well as at the state headquarters. We should not allow the continuance of the current Joint Secretary syndrome in New Delhi—which continues to suffer from personal egos and a compartmentalised vision of development of the country. If the group of ministers can sort out some of the vexed policy issues, similarly, Joint Secretaries too can form informal committees to resolve most of the file work moving from one desk to another. There are many interrelated issues, which should be resolved at a higher level of administration. This co-ordination and co-operation can further percolate down to the state and district levels. All these government efforts should be converged at the block-level.

With the help of IT, rural networking will provide a live and continuous dialogue between different sectors and policy makers who have a direct dialogue with the farmers, rural artisans and complement one another in making the rural economy a vehicle of change and development in the global perspective.

Rural Areas

As many as 29 subjects have been earmarked in our Constitution to be in the list of rural and local bodies purview. Thus we have now three lists of areas for the federal government, the state governments and local bodies respectively. However, most of the states so far have not taken effective steps to transfer these powers to the local bodies.

The reluctance of the state authorities to transfer these powers to the rural and local bodies is perhaps due to the perspective that the rural areas have traditionally been taken as caste-ridden, illiterate, poverty stricken and with squalor all around, poor in terms of basic infrastructure such as electricity, drinking water, etc. So, the people in these areas do not have the strength and education to take over the responsibilities of the 21 subjects earmarked for them, many think.

Is it not in contrast with the glamourised beautiful rural India, we sometimes see either in films or television? But what is the truth? Both are extremes—neither is rural India as bad as we believe nor as colourful as depicted in the films. But one thing is certain—the potential of rural India is yet to be marketed as the rural people do not have the necessary tools to market themselves effectively. They have a lot of untapped latent strength and they have huge potential of investible power of organisation. While some of these powers are known, but about most of them, we continue to be ignorant. It is also true that a large number of them have become victims of the so-called modern developments, but most of them have survived despite being threatened. If this latent strength of our people could be harnessed, the present hopeless situation might really take a U-turn.

Fortunately, at Cancun, Mr. Jaitley has succeeded in buying some time for us, but we cannot really postpone the pressures and pulls of the developed world. India must harness its resources and evolve a strategy to face the WTO pressures. With the opening of our economy, we have little option, but to accept marketing as the key area for any sustainable process of development. The rural areas so far have failed to market themselves with a very comprehensive strategy. It should not be a very narrow approach to marketing, which has already inflicted a lot of harm to our rural products. There is an urgent need to revise our developmental strategies, which so far have not really been able to deliver. The marketing has to be multi-dimensional marketing of place, product, concepts, ideas, vision, problems, processes, systems and even intentions.

Convergence

India's Mahalanobis model worked quite well till the Third Plan period. If the information technology as an important tool of administration and development had been there during the early years of our independence, India's economy might have been one of the world's robust economies. The Internet might have provided the much-needed one window approach to the vast countryside. However, in the industrial sector, the government has successfully been a provider through the one-window approach. The vast industries in the western sector are a living example of this approach. However, no such attempt has so far been made to evolve a *convergence* concept for rural development. *Convergence requires clarity and brevity to make it speedily accessible to the masses.* It is possible to reach the specific target groups through this approach with the help of new technologies. While convergence of single window services to the organised big industries can be a reality, when it comes to rural areas the convergence and efficient single window service continues to be a mirage.

All talk of development, especially for the organised masses in the unaccessible scattered rural India, continues to be a myth. Development means many things to many people. If the meaning of development is taken only in a narrow sense of little financial gain or some improvement in lifestyles, it is worth examining how much really have we gained or lost in this development process. Although some claim that the financial gains so far have been quite worthwhile, many justifiably feel that our development has been lopsided and even, in some cases, in reverse gear. In terms of happiness, satisfaction, contentment and overall quality of life, we definitely have not made progress. Therefore, the issues of economic growth, physical development, spiritual and cultural attainments etc. have to be examined holistically.

All this can be attained with the new technologies, but we have to evolve a mindset for all this.

Dimension of Delivery Systems in Rural Areas

It will be quite repetitive, if we look at a historical perspective of public service delivery system or reorientation of delivery system for production, services, administrative, educational sectors etc. The current system of development, which is totally dependent upon government employees, has so far failed to take off. Therefore, as policy formulators, we should be clear in our minds that any system, which does not involve people in the management, planning and convergence, can never be successful. The results will be disastrous, if the questions of mobilising different service providers or delivery systems, management are left only to government servants and funds. In the planning era, the thrust has so far been on delivery through government staff.

The attached table has been prepared to bring out the details of the 29 subjects, the functions, existing performers, weaknesses, need for newness and proposed action plan through e-governance. This chart looks holistically in dimensions of missing linkages and how-e-governance would facilitate efficient administration.

Challenges of Our Time

- Massive awakening.
- Failure of past development models.
- Collapse of socialism, doubts on capitalism and unavoidability of humanism.
- Redundancy of established institutions.
- All round lack of faith-prevalent negativism.
- Dwindling resources of the State—Siphoning off state resources to unproductive activities.
- Overstaffing and poor work culture around the State organisations—It is true even in most of private sector issues related to better management.
- Neglect of community and traditional practices.
- Realisation that states cannot be held together on religious or armament factors.
- Massive codification of examples of failures and successes.
- Humanity and human rights becoming supreme.
- Compulsions of global vision and local action (GVALA).
- Awareness among women and the neglected/exploited groups.
- Insistence on money as being the biggest wealth at every level.
- Need for regional and local authorities to shoulder the responsibilities and play their legitimate role with transparency and viability.
- Poor infrastructure and attention to be paid to the unorganised, dispersed and decentralised sectors and acceptance of its harsh realities.
- Imperative need to involve people, community and all role players.

It will be clear that many of these challenges are unique and unparalled. There is no historical semblance and hence we have to look for new models for effective functioning, timely correction, self-supporting planning and research systems for using all the development potential to face the disasters effectively.

E-Governance: An effective tool

When we look at India with special reference to rural areas, compulsions of convergence, sustainable development, marketing and delivery systems in rural areas as a part of challenges of our time, we find that the issues of holistic training, shift from charity to commerce, policy issues for self-employment and rural investment, rewards as per performance, optimisation of local resources, learning from the past and developing models for replication become very very important.

The emphasis of State-led extension, godown, infrastructure, training, marketing, production and many other areas have made people totally dependent on the State. One feels that the *whole confidence and capacity of self-employment has withered away.* Obviously, if all these have happened then policies of the State whether of policing, funding, rewarding, punishing etc. etc. cannot be forgotten. Their lessons compulsorily make it imperative for us by enhancing the efficiency of the delivery systems.

In many progressive states, the dependency syndrome on the government has reduced. Many companies as a part of aggressive marketing have developed their dealers and stockists to provide LOW COST PRACTICAL CONSULTANCIES (LCPCs). This cadre of LCPCs has not only close proximity to the target group but also is always *willing to learn and experiment* with new developments in their respective fields. There are many important fields where potential of self-employment and rural investment (SERI) needs to be suitably encouraged through policy support.

Lessons from the Past

Whether it is economic, social or any sector, we find specially with reference to rural areas the delivery systems *have been managed, funded, trained and monitored by a compartmentalised Joint Secretary Syndrome.* The Panchayat Raj institution now for the first time has been enjoined upon to ensure convergence. States like Uttar Pradesh have gone one step ahead and tried to pool various rural functionaries into single window service providers. This has *been done without increasing any manpower or even budget but by effective convergence.* Earlier 10-12 villages used to be serviced by one functionary and in total there were about 10-12 departments having their functionary for group of villages. By just convergence, now one village has one or two service providers who attend to 10-12 departments functions *at the village level.* Many objections have been raised. But the fact remains that if systems *have to be managed and not manipulated all the time then it is high time to understand* convergence for effectiveness in rural areas. Secondly, the work level and expertise *required at village level is so basic that no specialised service provider is required.* In case more people are needed, the panchayat can hire them. These will definitely lead to real *gram swaraj if the following aspects are not neglected:*

1. Holistic training.
2. Shift from charity to commerce.
3. Let people think about their development.
4. Self-employment and rural lives.
5. Rewards as per performance.
6. Local resources utilisation.
7. Quality products services and local demand.
8. Clarity of convergence, bankability, quality and effectiveness of technology.
9. Continuously learning from the past.
10. Developing clusters, rural godowns and building up local expertise on the principles of global vision and local action (GVALA).
11. Paying attention to Hidden Investible Power Potential Organisation (HIPPO), Known Investible Power Potential Organisation (KIPPO) and Threatened Investible Power Potential Organisation (TIPPO), and Frightening Investible Power Potential Organisation (FIPPO) regularly.
12. By neglecting traditional expertise and importance of local servicing at low cost, a lot of harm has been done.
13. Organisations of the rural poor have hardly received scientific attention. Capacity and capability of the caste systems have also to be redefined and relooked.
14. Role of local leaders developed in the last decades must shift from grants to business or greed to equity. Here policies can play a very important role.

15. Some hope generating signals or parameters have to be continuously searched. Can one believe that in UP there are thousands of villages where no law and order problem has been reported? Can one believe that no incentive rewards or even a good work has ever been done by anybody? The areas of *rewarding good work needs to be understood.*
16. The permanent civil services and their work culture with reference to convergence of delivery systems in rural areas needs to be studied from the grassroots. By encouraging the State to take up all duties and creation of the cadre of government employees, with their powerful unions, hardly any justice has been done to low cost high impact (LCHI) system development. Even voluntary system organisations have not remained aloof from this disease.
17. Overdependency on the State for everything cannot be changed overnight. The policies have been such that dependency always pays. Even not returning a bank loan is acclaimed. But now is the right time to ensure reversal of this process through suitable policies or transparency and incentives. Where are the group rewards or group punishments?

Since Independence, bureaucratic interference in the pretext of development has increased manifold but since 1990s liberalisation increased.

Panchayati Raj has a very important role to play. Hence all systems must be organised and geared to make them functional, progressive, analysable and capable of taking all steps of confidence building in all areas. Panchayats have been looked upon as the exploitative systems extension. *It is high time that the panchayat as an important partner in constitutional governance at the lowest level is accepted. This means effective decentralisation, delegation, funding and encouragement to converge with better policy and training prescriptions.* There is a growing realisation at many levels but the crux of the problem is *how to go about it?* For example, when it comes to law and order or policing, are we prepared to encourage those villages which have a crime free record for many decades? Or if some villages have no record of disease or bad recovery then are we prepared to encourage them? In the same way with reference to unemployment, population, development, godowns, infrastructure, swavalamban, swabhiman, are we prepared to delegate? Can our laws, rules, regulations be changed to make them totally empowered? *Isn't it a fact that nobody wants to share the power and authority? Hence can we now think of making things hot through effective accountability and responsibility fixation so that institutions are forced to delegate and share with panchayats not only resources but also accountability?* Can the good performing rural institutions of community, of village, of group be encouraged to resort to self-help? Can funding system be so developed that performance is encouraged and non-performance is punished? How do we look into issues of LEARNING TO WORK TOGETHER WITH TRANSPARENCY, BANKABILITY, VIABILITY AND RIGHT ATTITUDE? The systems of transfer of knowledge or systems where *ashram vyavastha* was ensuring continuity of training research, irrespective of caste and creed, needs to be examined. The element of suitability or *patrata* as pursued *by the teacher needs to be researched.* Can there be *volunteers as teachers* so that the missing linkages of personality development, decision taking capacity, continuous upgradation of ability to visualise challenges and develop systems for uninterrupted upgradation and transfer of knowledge in all walks of life is possible? These questions have to be looked into today as a part of the covergence of delivery systems for rural areas to face all types of disasters.

WHAT NEEDS TO BE DONE AND HOW OR PRESCRIPTION FOR CONVERGENCE OF DELIVERY SERVICES IN RURAL AREAS

1. Having analysed different aspects and urgency of convergence of delivery system in rural areas with reference to the challenges of our time and the aspirations of people, it is now the right time to attend to the action plan. Hence, words like clarity, brevity and speed have to be understood with reference to all the analysis done above. Due to lack of clarity, the brevity is not visible and automatically the speed of reform is missing. Hence *panchayati raj institutions, howsoever good or bad,*

they may have to be actively immediately and clearly involved in all the convergence plans.

2. Responsibility has to go with accountability. It is here that the role of policies of funding, training, marketing, rewarding, incentive providing, electing and even propelling has to have an element of performance based rewards. Once difficult programmes are identified, there should be no problem in suitably *developing reward systems.*
3. Ultimately if the Panchayats have to achieve GRAM SWARAJ and sustainable win-win situation for all, then they have to involve local expertise, local resources and talents for solving their problems. The building up of the capacity to analyse and visualise has to be a part of the empowerment process.
4. Various *models are available.* They need to be churned, examined, holistically researched and then depending upon local conditions taken *up for replication.* This is not the job of government or government dependent NGOs. The people and the representatives through panchayat have to be involved to take up the challenges of implementation.
5. If the target group is analysed properly then there should be no problem in a sensitised bureaucracy to change policies to empower people. Liberalisation makes it imperative that state funded programmes and priorities become market oriented thrust areas. Hence low cost practical consultants (LCPCs) have to be trained through information technology. This will solve the problem of self-employment, non-performing assets (NPAs) and also create conditions where self-supporting systems get propelled on a sustainable basis.
6. The State has not looked after work culture, motivation, inspiration of the staff. By tempering a few services, the actual workers at cutting edge level have remained neglected. This has resulted in indifference to the people and lack of confidence in the masses. Hence, rural convergence by local leadership can solve these problems.
7. All established institutions have to relook into the question of why they should stay together, work together or think together. The element of benefit, urgency to live together, the compulsions of understanding through holistic analysis etc. is

the urgency of the time. When more and more groups, institutions, communities want to get segregated and hope to better their lot through separation, the invariable question of why should people or state stay together needs research. When 'I' is becoming supreme and tolerance level going down, this question needs to be examined from the ultimate aim of life, or governance or even the objective of any change mission.

8. Once urgency of convergence, transparency, right to information, accountability, self-employment, viable investment, effective servicing of the unorganised, etc. are realised then local expertise must be tapped. This means the attitude and analytical capacity development of the rural leaders. One should not hesitate to say that our training institutions and trainers have hardly succeeded in achieving this capability of solving the problem through local resources.
9. As mentioned earlier, the role of policies will be very very crucial in ensuring the convergence effectively at the rural level. There can be no fixed or stereotyped prescriptions for convergence and hence as per *local conditions, capacity, limitations, aspirations and experiences of the past* alongwith the type of leadership it should be possible to have quick or slow convergence of delivery system. In some states and areas, total convergence is possible, justifiable and required. While in areas and programmes where dependency on the State has been massive, the process of convergence would obviously be slow and tedious. Needless to say, with better training systems, communication, sharing of resources and knowledge, and effective tools for conviction, there should be no delay in effective convergence, leading to that quality of life which everyone is looking for.
10. For many things time is the right prescription. When we look holistically at various dimensions of development, we find that the urgency or convergence of delivery systems for rural areas is absolutely ripe in all dimensions. Some obstacles, which have been mentioned above, can also be got over easily with right brainstorming and sensitisation.
11. Time and tide wait for none. India is a very fortunate country where the traditional and the modern can be blended. The

element of *DADI* (*Dwindling Accepted Down Investment*) is still very much to be seen and felt. The low cost high impact traditional practitioners of various convergable programmes, when properly involved, can definitely achieve that super quality of life. The simple people, the simple solutions, simple technologies are to be involved with the simple policies in the convergence of delivery systems.

12. In the process of convergence, priority must be given to the following factors:

    (i) Internal resource generation,
    (ii) Population control,
    (iii) Basic education,
    (iv) Self employment,
    (v) Value addition of rural raw material and local storage,
    (vi) Law and order free village or no litigation or no FIR,
    (vii) Recognition of sportsmen and artists,
    (viii) Rural resources utilisation, NRI involvement, exports, total literacy, women institutions and cooperatives,
    (ix) Programmes for senior citizens,
    (x) Environmental factors like plantation, bio-fertilisers and utilisation of neem, tulsi, herbals, local skills etc., and
    (xi) Utilisation of surplus land.

    Apart from the above financial points, reward for peace and stability, election free selections, GDP enhancement, planning with bank finance, litigation free redressal of grievances, convergence of resources, sports, culture, arts, competitions, single window services to people, village planning, recovery of bank loans, accountability, transparency, welfare of all, involvement of NRIs, self employment and resource mobilisation from MP fund, MLA fund etc. etc. may help a lot in developing a totally new work culture and new leadership.

13. In the era of liberalisation and the general agreement on trade and tariff, and with the *opening up of the economy, the role of decentralised governance has to be strongly recommended, appreciated and implemented. There is bound to be resistance.* The ability to manage, with refreshing freshness is the need of

the time. Harsh issues have to be faced squarely. There is nobody to share the pain, but with better planning, training, mind setting and understanding of tangible and intangible, it is possible to get away from the inefficiency led development model of yester years. The unorganised sector is ready to accept the challenges. What is immediately required are *the right policies, questioning of the outdated systems and procedures, local answers and local questions, sustainable models, involvement of grandmother and convergence in all respect.* Development challenges require self-employment oriented, training modules not only for NGOs, government servants but also for politicians at all levels. *The question of "effective" has to be understood in the right perspective. If needs appreciation of democratic values and adjustment of differences, issues in living together, working together for peace and gender issues, understanding conditions and spiritual dimensions of development, ego and recognition, differences and discipline, image and globalisation, commodities and differences, livelihood and luxuries, mentality of questioning and don't believe attitude, shaping up of policies and replication with local resources, business orientation and oxygen points for motivating the people, the community and ultimately identifying issues of self-actualisation, historical base of the society and challenges of tomorrow as a part of holistic and continuous development.*

To sum up

It would be absolutely clear that realising the dream of efficient administration through e-governance is very much a possibility. With little policy corrections through sensitised mindsets and performing systems development, the efficiency in administration with reduced cost and enhanced reliability is very much realisable.

12

Development of Rural Clusters

A Task Force, set up by Planning Commission on Employment Strategies and Employment Monitoring at State Level under the Chairmanship of Dr. S.P. Gupta, the then Member, Planning Commission, has recommended targeting ten million employment opportunities per year over the Tenth Five Year Plan period. Of this, 9.26 million is proposed to be from primary sector, 14.48 million from secondary and 25.26 million from the tertiary sector. Of the secondary sector, 10.14 million is proposed to be generated through programme based activities like *KVIC* (Khadi & Village Industries Commission), PMRY and SSI clusters and growth based activities under SSI and traditional non farm activities. In this connection a *concept paper* outlining the association of National Bank for Agriculture and Rural Development (NABARD) in the generation of employment creation and skill development through clusters and how to go about with this programme.

It may be noted that NABARD, on its establishment, decided to give a thrust to the development of non-farm sector with a view to increase the employment opportunities in the rural areas, considering the lesser prospects of creating additional employment in the agriculture sector. Accordingly, it had set up seven Task Forces to study the traditional sectors like Khadi, sericulture, coir, handloom, handicrafts, village industries, and marketing. Based on their reports, it introduced a new set of refinance schemes only to support the rural non-farm sector. Over the years, these schemes were refined and also new products were introduced to give a boost to the sector.

STUDIES INITIATED BY NABARD FOR PROMOTING RURAL NON-FARM SECTOR

A Committee was set up under Shri Vijay Mahajan in 1994, which was funded jointly by Swiss Development Cooperation and NABARD, to study the current situation, the constraints and potentials of rural non-farm sector with a view to evolve suitable package for policy and institutional intervention. The study has thrown open a number of strategies on which RNFS could be promoted in the country.

First of all, the study team endorsed the view of Dr. T.S. Tapola of Planning Commission, who had indicated that employment in rural non-farm sector grew at a faster rate than agriculture sector. As against 0.77 per cent growth in employment in agriculture during 1977 to 1988, the non-agriculture sector grew by 5.4 per cent. Thus, achievement of goal of full employment could be possible only by promoting rural non-farm sector. Further, it observed that apart from contributing to the goal of full employment, there are other benefits of promoting the rural non-farm sector such as increased income for rural workers, building up skill-base of rural population, lower capital intensity in terms of the capital labour and capital output ratios, lower commercial energy requirements for the same level of value added, lower use of imported inputs including petroleum products and a high contribution to exports.

As per the 1991 census, 2.6 per cent of the rural main workers in the Rural Small and Micro Enterprise (RSME) sector were engaged in mining, 32.2 per cent in manufacturing and repairs, 5.9 per cent in construction, 18.5 per cent in trade, 7 per cent in transport and 33.8 per cent in other services. Growth rates of rural employment in the 9 aggregate industrial categories computed for the period 1981-1991 showed that the overall growth rate of RSME sector workers was 2.7 per cent per annum comprising of 2.5 per cent in mining, 2.6 per cent in non-household manufacturing, 2.3 per cent in construction, 3.7 per cent in trade, 1.3 per cent in transport and 4.5 per cent in other services. The top ten sub-sectors with high employment share based on NSS data for 1987-88 were construction (14.6 per cent), retail trade in food and beverages (11.5 per cent), public administration (6.4 per cent), personal services (6.0 per cent), land transport (5.5 per cent), textile products (5.5 per cent), manufacture of wood products (5.1 per cent), educational services (4.6 per cent), manufacture of tobacco and beverages (4.1 per cent) and cotton textiles (4.1 per cent).

Based on these findings, the Committee had identified some of the sectors and activities which could be promoted for realising higher employment growth in the country. These sectors were divided into emergent sub-sectors, high growth sub-sectors and high share sub-sectors.

Emergent Sub-Sectors

These are sub-sectors which at present support relatively little employment but which have potential for growth in the near future because of unmet demand. These sub-sectors usually emerge in response to rapidly growing niche markets, often export demand and are based on hitherto underutilised raw materials and skills. Examples of such emergent sub-sectors are fruit processing and granite processing in Andhra Pradesh, agro services and rural transport in Assam, readymade garmets, cement ware and small engineering in Gujarat, tussar silk, fish processing and rural tourism in Orissa, food processing and rural business in Punjab, minor minerals, leather and rural tourism in Rajasthan, sericulture and rural tourism in Tamil Nadu and fruit and herbal processing and rural transport in Uttar Pradesh.

High Growth Sub-Sectors

These are sub-sectors which have registered high growth rate of employment due to demand in the domestic and/or the export market. Examples of these types of sub-sectors are silk textiles and repairs in Andhra Pradesh, fibre products and construction in Assam, textile and cement products in Gujarat, spice processing and rural tourism in Orissa, freight transport and metalware in Punjab, oil seeds processing and handicrafts in Rajasthan, powerlooms and hosiery in Tamil Nadu and leather products and pottery in Uttar Pradesh.

High Share Sub-Sectors

These are sub-sectors which at present account for a high share of employment in this sector even though the demand prospects for some are uncertain. Examples of these types of sub-sectors are paddy processing and manufacture of Bidis in Andhra Pradesh, cane and wood products and handlooms in Assam, food products and pottery in Gujarat, fish processing in Orissa, grain milling and brick manufacture in Punjab, gem processing in Rajasthan, matches in Tamil Nadu and carpet weaving in Uttar Pradesh.

The Committee concluded the report by saying that rural small and micro enterprise sector in India has a promise of becoming the most dynamic part of economy, rural or urban. It has the possibility to absorb as many as 45 million new entrants to the employment market out of nearly 100 million who would be unemployed in the next decade.

NABARD's Role in Promoting Rural Non-Farm Sector

The above studies as well as other numerous studies, workshops and meets conducted in-house by NABARD have been able to give a focus to promotion of rural non-farm sector. As a result of all these, NABARD has been able to refine its policies for supporting RNFS, leading to a refinance support of over Rs. 9100 crore for rural non-farm sector enabling establishment of 18 lakh production units and creation of 60 lakh employment opportunities.

Apart from the refinance support, NABARD has also been supporting various promotional agencies like NGOs/voluntary agencies/other developmental agencies in experimenting with various promotional activities supporting the development of rural non-farm sector, right from the late eighties. A number of promotional programmes like entrepreneurship development, skill development, facilitation/support institutions, marketing of products, gender development, micro-credit programmes, etc. have been supported. A total of over Rs. 44 crore have been spent as grant assistance for various promotional activities.

The major initiatives are District Rural Industries Project (DRIP), Rural Entrepreurship Development Programme (REDP), and Cluster Development. Based on the past experience, it was felt that adopting an area approach and within the area, commodity/ sector approach, could make credit more effective and result-oriented. Since 'district' is the basic unit for planning in the government, linkages and infrastructure support for development can be better ensured if the district as a whole is selected for planning and development. Incidentally, NABARD itself prepares Potential Linked Credit Plans (PLCPs) on a district basis. Besides, the governmental extension agencies have negligible presence in the rural industrial sector, at block level and below, unlike agriculture. Hence, it is proposed to experiment large area based scheme on a district basis for development of rural non-farm sector (RNFS).

Encouraged by the success achieved in some districts and keeping in view the overwhelming support received from all the project partners in the development of RNFS in these districts, NABARD has extended the project to 74 more districts in a phased manner. Thus at present the project is under implementation in 80 districts spread over 19 states. NABARD has also decided to extend its coverage to more number of districts in the coming years in a phased manner.

Besides the above efforts, NABARD has been able to identify 65 clusters and launched 55 of them as part of National Programme of Rural Industrialisation (NPRI) introduced by the Government of India.

NABARD adopted Clusters

NABARD is actively involved in the implementation of the National Programme for Rural Industrialisation (NPRI). Fifty five clusters spread over 18 states have been taken up for development under the programme. The activities covered under cluster development could be broadly classified into artisan based, fruit processing, handicrafts and handlooms, silk weaving, sisal fibre rope making, leather craft, brass and bell metal, pottery, ceramic toys making, bamboo craft, etc. Financial assistance by way of grant is extended to nodal agencies/NGOs associated with the cluster development for implementing varied promotional programmes.

Importance of Clusters

The NABARD experience can be a model for NER micro enterprises in rural areas engaged in various economic activities individually. They find it difficult to operate economically, as they face stiff competition from each other as well as from the organised sector. Development of clusters helps in deriving benefits of economies of scale in procurement of raw materials, production and post-production operations.

"Cluster development approach" has emerged during the last decade as one of the effective development instruments, among industrially developed and developing countries, to enable the small scale enterprises to withstand the challenges thrown up by competition and globalisation.

Clusters have existed in India for centuries. It is estimated that there are around 350 modern small and medium enterprises (SMEs) clusters and about 2000 artisans-based rural clusters in India. NABARD has been advocating cluster approach to lending since long through its various programmes/schemes like District Rural Industries Project (DRIP), Mother Units, Common Service Centres, Artisan Guilds, etc. Integrated and flexible approach, collective and coordinated efforts in cluster development would result in emergence of innumerable and sustainable individual/group rural micro enterprises.

Objective of NABARD's cluster development approach

Strengthening of existing clusters and development of new clusters in exceptional cases towards sustainable competitive advantage through technology upgradation/transfer, raw material access, skill development, managerial inputs and credit support, market support.

Cluster Philosophy

- Focused assistance.
- Demand-based assistance.
- Flexible instruments of assistance to meet specific needs of cluster.

- Close monitoring to spur continuous development and innovation.

NABARD's Strategy

Cluster development encompasses all the vital inputs required for a successfully managed enterprise. NABARD follows a calibrated strategy which facilitates growth in terms of:

- Enterprise promotion and entrepreneurship development,
- Flow of institutional credit—provision of working capital,
- Employment generation, increase in income level,
- Backward and forward linkages,
- Government's support,
- Sustainability of enterprises/financial viability of clusters,
- Inter cluster business/relationship, and
- Vertical and horizontal integration of clusters and their replication.

Methodology

Preparation of Cluster Status-Bench mark

- Number of people/families employed,
- Nature of activity being undertaken,
- Age of the cluster,
- Source of raw material,
- Skill levels,
- Where and how products are marketed,
- Existing linkages,
- Existing arrangements for financial support from banks/private parties,
- Existence of local support organisations, and
- All other relevant details of the activity/product line.

Action Plan

An indepth **diagnostic study** of the activity identified for cluster development is conducted before any interventions are taken up in the cluster. The objective of the study is to generate crucial information about local conditions, employment (wage employment/ self-employment/contract employment/employment of women, direct/indirect employment), existing skills, potential for development of skills, number of artisans engaged in the activity, raw material, production process, products produced, usage of tools and machinery, design, quality control, credit needs of the artisans, infrastructure facilities, access to market (local, regional or national), specific needs for further development of the cluster, etc. Besides, critical features helping sectoral growth are also studied.

An **Action Plan** is prepared suitably addressing the critical areas identified in the diagnostic study and suggesting stage-wise action for a period of three years so that strategies for skill development, resource mobilisation, raw material supply, marketing, organisation and management etc. are taken up at appropriate stages.

Selection of nodal agency

A capable NGO/VA/any development agency is identified to associate in the implementation of specific promotional intervention for the development of the cluster. Activities, for which intervention by other agencies viz. State Government for creation of necessary infrastructure facilities, KVIC for establishing marketing network, etc. are brought out clearly so that related issues can be taken up with the agencies concerned. Efforts are made to dovetail the government schemes such as SGSY, Baba Saheb Ambedkar Hastshilp Vikas Yojana (AHVY) so as to ensure holistic development of the cluster.

Cluster level interventions envisage direct action to develop demonstrative models for attaining greater sustainability and competitiveness. Any marketing intervention should open the artisans and his products to the large commercial stream. Hence, NABARD is keen in facilitating strategic alliances with reputed business organisations/marketing organisations as well as exploring the possibilities for creation of brand name, standardisation of product and quality check, packaging, etc.

Financial assistance from NABARD

NABARD provides financial assistance by way of grant to the identified nodal agencies for implementing specific programmes required as suggested in the Action Plan for development of the cluster.

Purposes for which financial assistance from NABARD is available

- Conduct of diagnostic study/survey,
- Awareness/motivation programmes,
- Skill upgradation/market-oriented/entrepreneurial development programmes,
- Training of/by master craftsmen,
- Product development workshops,
- Establishment of Common Facility Centre (CFC),
- Engaging technical personnel/specialists,
- Organising exhibitions, buyer-seller meets,
- Publishing of cluster pamphlets/newsletter etc.,
- Administrative costs/overheads to the implementing nodal agency, and
- Any other specific intervention required for development of the cluster eligible for NABARD assistance.

Follow up and Monitoring-Data Base

Like NABARD, which through its Regional offices and District Development offices effectively follow up and monitor the implementation of the cluster development programme, besides attempting to build database in respect of each of the NABARD adopted cluster, can be followed by NEC and State Governments of NER.

Field study of NABARD adopted clusters

The **summary of the findings** of the field study revealed that NABARD's s promotional interventions and its role as facilitator in coordinating with various agencies in the clusters have resulted in:

- Attitudinal change in the beneficiaries who are now motivated for achieving socio-economic development of the cluster,
- Awareness of opportunities for furthering their cluster activity,
- Gender Equity,

- Formation of artisans' associations in most of the clusters to facilitate the power of collective bargaining,
- Improvement in the level of technology and skill upgradation,
- Product development in terms of quality control and range of products,
- Gainful employment and sustainable income generation,
- Revival of handicrafts as a profitable source of employment,
- One hundred SHGs were formed to provide access to bank credit by linking them to formal banking system,
- Bank credit to the tune of Rs. 2 crore disbursed in these clusters,
- Repayment ethics inculcated among the beneficiaries,
- Assisting the beneficiaries in direct marketing and exposure to the latest trends,
- Export of cluster products and participation in international exhibitions,
- Income pattern of the cluster members reveals 50-100 per cent increase in the post-intervention period,
- Additional employment for 3400 people generated in these clusters helped in arresting migration from rural clusters to urban areas, and
- Two thousand new units were set up in these clusters encouraged by the success of NABARD's promotional programmes.

13

Impact of the NABARD Initiative

Poverty Alleviation

- Majority of the beneficiaries in NABARD clusters fall in 'BPL' (Below Poverty Line).
- The income pattern of the cluster members in the pre- and post-intervention periods reveals 50-100 per cent increase.
- NABARD's coordination with DRDA and other government departments helped in dovetailing its cluster development programme with government schemes such as Swarna Jayanti Gram Swarozgar Yojana (SGSY) and Babasaheb Ambedkar Hastashilp Vikas Yojana (AHVY) for maximising support to the cluster through convergence of efforts of all possible agencies.

Employment Generation

- Artisans who were unemployed/underemployed are gainfully employed after adoption of clusters by NABARD.
- There has been an increase in production as new units have been set up in the clusters with easy availability of bank credit.

Women Empowerment

- Gender equity achieved through mobilisation of women into Self-Help Groups.
- Self-Help Group formation has brought out the latent leadership quality in women and boosted their self confidence. Women confined to their households earlier are now aware of savings, maintenance of accounts and banking and knowledge

of the intricacies of the cluster activity—right from purchase of raw material to sale of the finished products which were hitherto unknown to them.

Improving access to credit

- Most of the cluster artisans were caught in the vicious cycle of indebtedness as money lenders were the sole source of credit before NABARD entered the area.
- Today the beneficiaries are out of the clutches of money lenders who lent at usurious rates of interest ranging from 3 per cent to 10 per cent per month.
- For many beneficiaries visiting a bank was a dream never to be fulfilled. With NABARD's efforts the cluster members are now confidently approaching bankers.
- Awareness/motivation programmes to bankers at the district level organised by NABARD has changed the attitude of bankers as well.
- NABARD's liaison with commercial banks, cooperative banks, RRBs in the district has proved helpful to cluster beneficiaries to avail of need-based credit.

Repayment Ethics

- The noteworthy feature is inculcateion of repayment ethics by NABARD.
- Many of the artisans were defaulters before NABARD stepped into the cluster but now repayment by artisans is prompt and regular.
- Its intervention has resulted in better end-use of credit.

Common Facility Centres and Technology Upgradation

- Common facility centres have been set up at most of the clusters either with NABARD grant or under SGSY Infrastructure Fund.
- Essential machinery provided for CFC by NABARD in the clusters has aided in
  –reduction of drudgery,

–enhanced production levels,
–enhanced productivity, and
–better quality.

Skill Upgradation

- In most of the NABARD clusters, the activity being traditional, age old methods were followed.
- NABARD has conducted several skill upgradation, rural entrepreneurship development, product development, design development and product diversification programmes through experienced and renowned agencies such as National Institute of Design, National Institute of Fashion Technology, Small Industries Service Institute, Regional Design and Technology Development Centre, Bangalore, Srishti School of Art and Craft, Bangalore, etc.

Marketing

- The artisans in the cluster were exploited by middlemen in the pre-intervention period.
- NABARD has assisted all the cluster artisans to participate in local fairs, state level and national level exhibitions.
- Grant was given for exposure visits to other places/clusters to learn new techniques and diversify into new products for wider market base.
- Such participation has exposed the rural artisans to the latest market trends, consumer preferences and importance of quality to fetch better prices.
- Assessment of market is helping the artisans refine their products in terms of quality, range and fixing the prices of cluster products based on demand.
- Buyer-seller meets organised for direct marketing.
- Grant assistance is being provided by NABARD for market surveys. Such surveys help in identifying the potential for the products and know the pulse of different buyers and search new avenues for marketing.
- The nodal agencies of NABARD are trying to tap export markets and have succeeded in few clusters.

Impediments

Encountered by the beneficiaries brought out by the field level studies conducted by NABARD

1. Non availability of working capital

Most of the cluster members are denied bank credit as they are earlier defaulters. Formation of SHGs by NABARD has solved this problem to a large extent. However, in some cases banks are not willing to finance groups with members who are defaulters. In some areas, it is very difficult to persuade bankers to lend working capital loan for the cluster activity as the artisans do not have any stocks to pledge. Most of the NABARD clusters being artisan based, the handicraft items do not find ready market and thus the artisans are affected, as they do not get funds for purchase of raw material immediately.

2. Marketing

Though reduced to a large extent, presence of middlemen still exists. Their presence is becoming inevitable in certain clusters as the artisans depend on them to sell their products as they don't find a ready market for their handicrafts/products. The artisans are supplied with raw material by these traders/middlemen who buy their products at very cheap rates and sell them at exorbitant rates cornering all the profit. In the process, the artisans don't fetch the remuneration due to them. *To continue the activity, continuous flow of funds is required. Since the artisans don't get credit for working capital they are unable to hold the products till they fetch a better price.* NABARD grant for exhibitions/fairs/melas have giving lot of exposure to our cluster artisans to understand market demand and assess the latest consumer preferences as they come into contact directly with the buyers. However, some of the cluster artisans have expressed their inability to meet the existing demand for such exhibitions as they are not able to purchase raw material to the required extent.

3. Clarity of roles of partner agencies

Cluster development is essentially a convergence of efforts of all development agencies, bankers and other business development service providers to obtain optimum benefit for the socio-economic progress of the clusters. However, it is observed that in many clusters, instead of playing complementary roles, the partner agencies are duplicating the efforts in an eagerness to take credit for the development.

4. Health care for artisans

Certain activities like horn and bone craft involve very hazardous health conditions on account of the foul smell emanated from the raw material depot and emission of dust during grinding which is harmful to the artisans. For instance, in the horn and bone craft cluster at Moradabad, 80 per cent of the artisans are suffering from TB. NABARD could provide safety kit consisting of helmets, goggles, masks and hand gloves to some artisans which had demonstration effort on the others who also started using safety kits. Government should consider providing medical facilities exclusively for such clusters wherein high hazardous working conditions prevail.

5. Ignorance among district officials

In most of the clusters it is observed that District Level Implementing Committee (DLIC) to be formed under NPRI for monitoring the cluster development programme is not in place and some of the District Industries Centres (DICs) are not aware of the fact that the DLIC is to be convened by them. This is one of the reasons for non-cooperation by various government departments in the cluster. It is observed that only those clusters where all the partners cooperate with the implementing agencies of NPRI have recorded remarkable progress. The need for involvement of all the concerned district authorities and officials will go a long way in successful cluster development programme in identified clusters.

14

Tribute to Gandhi

It is difficult to usualize any holistic development without recollecting Mahatma Gandhi's concept of development.

Gandhi's Talisman

"I will give you a talisman. Whenver you are in doubt or when the self becomes too much with you, apply the following test.

Recall the face of the poorest and the weakest man whom you may have seen and ask yourself if the step you contemplate is going to be of any use to him. Will he gain anything by it? Will it restore him to control over his own life and destiny? In other words, will it lead to Swaraj for the hungry and spiritually starving millions?

Then you will find your doubts and your self melting away."

During his nearly eight months study leave with Indian Institute of Public Administration (IIPA). Dr. Kamal Taori had the opportunity of studying holistic issues with a Gandhian perspective. The development and disaster have wider implications because of persistent failure of building up grassroots institutions and community-based organisations.

The present compartmentalised structure of governance, funding, policy making, technology transfer and even training does not inspire convergenistic processes leading to shift from charity to creativity, capacity and confidence building of the people. Based upon discussion, study of literature, persistent neglect of issues of empowerment of the people, it was found that a fresh look is needed on these issues.

The dwindling resources of the State and lack of the necessary initiatives in the institutions surrounding the society a time has come to take a holistic look. Government of India has 50 Ministries and total about 90 departments. The Joint Secretary system of work distribution may be alright when it comes to law and order or regulatory type of system of governance. But when it comes to people-friendly, cost-effective, transparent, right to information-oriented convergenistic systems, there is need to relook and explore this system. With the rising expectations of the masses if efforts are not made it will invariably result in further catastrophe and loss of confidence leading to chaotic disastrous situation.

Why strengthen the grassroots governance through panchayats?

While analysing the trends of the past happenings during the present and their impact on the future developmental scenario, the conclusion seems to be a holistic, multi-dimensional plan of action. The issues of professionalism with social economic reconstruction and volunteering needed to be looked into from the angle of employment generation specially the self-employment, emerging viable investment opportunity, role of IT and how policies could strengthen or weaken the fabric of the society. Optimising the availability and impact of the scarce resources in an otherwise greed-led systems shrouded with secrecy and mystery needs to be dismystified. The focus on grassroots governance whether of villages or township opens up challenging opportunities specially after 73rd and 74th Amendment to the Constitution. The 29 subjects earmarked for Panchayats have also not been effectively handed over. While some states have handed over the functions, but the financial controls continue with them. The realisation of doing justice to the grassroots governance is very much visible but not in action. The decentralised, non-farm, unorganised, rural-based sectors offer challenging opportunity for facing the multi-dimensional problems of pollution, poverty, environmental degradation, unemployment and on the whole all that which makes society poorly and miserably performing. However, now there is no doubt that all have accepted the need for urgency of strengthening and galvanising the rural instutitions.

Role of NGOs, Community Based Organisations and Panchayats

Needless to say that the issues of challenges of our time, persistent realities and compulsions of democratic systems of governance require locally resource-based initiatives. Here the role of training, introspection, rewards and incentives have to be practical, affordable and replicable. By neglecting the community-based organisations, tremendous harm is being inflicted on the concept of State and good governance itself.

29 Subjects for Panchayats and problem of attitude mindset accountability and neglect of human resource development

1. Agriculture including agricultural extension,
2. Land improvement, implementation of land reforms, land consolidation and soial conservation,
3. Minor irrigation, water management and watershed development,
4. Animal husbandry, dairying and poultry,
5. Fisheries,
6. Social forestry and farm forestry,
7. Minor forest produce,
8. Small scale industries, including food processing industries,
9. Khadi, village and cottage industries,
10. Rural housing,
11. Drinking water,
12. Fuel and fodder,
13. Roads, culverts, bridges, ferries, waterways and other means of communication,
14. Rural electrification, including distribution of electricity,
15. Non-conventional energy sources,
16. Poverty alleviation programme,
17. Education, including primary and secondary schools,
18. Technical training and vocational education,
19. Adult and non-formal education,
20. Libraries,
21. Cultural activities,
22. Markets and fairs,

23. Health and sanitation, including hospitals, primary health centres and dispensaries,
24. Family welfare,
25. Women and child development,
26. Social welfare, including welfare of the handicapped and mentally retrarded,
27. Welfare of the weaker sections, and in particular, of the scheduled castes and the scheduled tribes,
28. Public distribution system, and
29. Maintenance of community assets.

The IT has a crucial role in the convergence of delivery systems in rural areas for self-employment and disaster management and empowerment of community

With the advent of information technology, computers and their easy accessibility, tremendous power of the people can be unleashed. The issues of convergence, reliability, transparency, easy affordability, consistency, cost-effective marketing and enhancing viability with infrastructure development could be a reality. The role of policies whether in funding, pricing, technology transfer or employment could all be harnessed to bring out the best of the real India.

Index